The Guide to Grammar

A Student Handbook for Strong Writing

By Laura Wilson

 Maupin House *by*

capstone®
professional

The Guide to Grammar: A Student Handbook for Strong Writing
By Laura Wilson

Cover Design: Sandra D'Antonio

Book Design: Jodi Pedersen

Library of Congress Cataloging-in-Publication Data
Wilson, Laura.
  The Guide to Grammar : A Student Handbook for Strong Writing /
by Laura Wilson.
        pages cm.
  Includes bibliographical references.
ISBN 978-1-62521-927-5 (pbk.)
ISBN 978-1-62521-937-4 (ebook PDF)
ISBN 978-1-62521-951-0 (ebook)
1. English language—Grammar—Study and teaching (Middle school)
2. English language—Composition and exercises—Study and teaching
(Middle school) I. Title.
  LB1631.W495 2015
  428.20712--dc23   2014006943

Maupin House publishes professional resources for K–12 educators. Contact us for
tailored, in-school training or to schedule an author for a workshop or conference.
Visit www.maupinhouse.com for free lesson plan downloads.

Maupin House Publishing, Inc. by Capstone Professional
1710 Roe Crest Drive
North Mankato, MN 56003
www.maupinhouse.com
888-262-6135
info@maupinhouse.com

Printed in the United States of America in Eau Claire, Wisconsin.
072718   000821

Dedication and Acknowledgments

I dedicate this book to an exceptional teacher: my mother, Linda Jacobson, whose grammar, teaching, and writing expertise inspired so many, especially her daughter.

First, I am grateful to have Melissa Slive, Devin Maduras, and Nina Auerbach by my side. These three incredible women make the impossible possible, and they make coming to work every day a joy. Second, to Aemilia Phillips, intern extraordinaire! Aemilia's writing creativity, verve, and voice helped add the sparkle to this book. I also want to thank all my students who make teaching a joy, as well as Emily Bloom, Ashley LaRue, Tim O'Brien, Brandon Shenkman, RuthAnn Cote, and Annalie Aplin. A special thanks to Karen Soll, Emily Raij, and Lynnette Brent.

Table of Contents

Introduction

Every day, you rely on grammar. You tell stories, share ideas, describe foods, give directions, and share your opinions without even thinking about grammar or sentence structure.

Then why can a blank page or computer screen, waiting to be filled with your thoughts, seem so scary at times? Because of gerunds, infinitives, clauses, oh my! Grammar can be intimidating. This book will give you a blueprint for writing—supplying you with easy-to-use tools and easy-to-remember tips that will help you construct strong sentences, allowing you to write anything and everything with skill and confidence! When you start with the basic sentence and learn how to add key grammar strategies and important elements of style, your writing will become as fluent and engaging as any story you tell aloud.

This book is meant not only to introduce you to the patterns found within writing but also to explain some basic (but essential) rules of grammar in a not-a-horrible-lesson-in-grammar type of way, so that **you** (pronoun) **will** (tense) **do** (verb) **well** (adverb) **at** (preposition) **writing** (noun)!

Good writing goes far beyond simply applying the rules of grammar. To be effective, writing must be clear, descriptive, interesting, and persuasive. After learning how to use these simple tools, you will effortlessly begin linking words into amazing sentences, sentences into paragraphs, and paragraphs into essays, stories, books, and more! Then that blank page that was once daunting will become exciting and inviting—waiting to be filled with your fantastic writing!

How to Use This Book

This book translates confusing grammar jargon and complex explanations into clear, concise, and memorable descriptions for middle school students. Starting with the simple sentence structure and the fundamental parts of speech as a foundation, students will learn to develop their writing by identifying and utilizing the key grammatical tools that build strong, confident writers.

Each chapter contains simple-to-understand explanations that illustrate essential grammatical rules. The book is divided into three sections: **Chapter 1: The Foundation, Chapter 2: Building a Great Sentence,** and **Chapter 3: Finishing Touches.** This organization logically takes the student, step by step, through the process of crafting powerful, dynamic sentences. Accompanying **practice sheets** (with **answer keys**) provide essential practice, and the **Nuts and Bolts Grammar Reference Guide** offers easy-to-remember tips in one convenient list.

Many students are afraid of writing. They look at a blank sheet of paper or an empty computer screen and panic, not knowing where to start, what to write, or how to express themselves. This book helps students get their ideas "on paper" clearly and eloquently. Even hesitant students will learn to quickly create sentences that are interesting and thought provoking, resulting in a well-written, standout body of work.

There are two ways to use this book:

1. Use this book as a handy reference guide—refer to specific chapters and lessons for grammar rules to apply when writing, and reinforce skills learned with the supplemental practice sheets.

2. Review the book chronologically—each chapter builds on the next. Start with learning how sentences are constructed (using parts of speech). Follow this up with learning how to modify a sentence and to turn the simple sentence into a compound, complex, or compound/complex sentence. End with focusing on elements of style and turning sentences into cohesive, dynamic writing.

As a final note, this book aligns with the new Common Core State Standards for English Language Arts for fifth through eighth grade, serving as a resource to both teachers and students.

Your Grammar Toolbox: A No-Nonsense Reference Page

Just as you need tools to build a house, you need the parts of speech to build a well-constructed sentence. Below are the grammatical tools that will help you build strong sentences.

The parts of speech are words that construct sentences:

1. **Nouns:** People, places, or things—the subject of the sentence (See page 10.)

2. **Pronouns:** Substitutes for nouns (*I, he, she, they, it,* etc.) (See page 12.)

3. **Adjectives:** Descriptions of nouns or pronouns (See page 34.)

4. **Verbs:** Action words (See page 18.)

5. **Adverbs:** Descriptions of verbs or adjectives, usually ending in *-ly* (See page 36.)

6. **Conjunctions:** Joining or linking words (*and, or, but, nor,* etc.) (See page 45.)

7. **Prepositions:** Little words that give position (See page 39.)

8. **Interjections:** Words or phrases used to exclaim, protest, or command (See page 41.)

To build something special within your writing, you will also need:

Transitions: Link ideas and allow the reader to prepare for a reversal or continuation in thought (See page 75.)

Comparisons: Usually involve "as" or "than" and have to be equal on each side (See page 49.)

Phrases: "Wannabe" sentences that just aren't quite there—such as a group of words, without a subject or a verb, that functions in a sentence as a single part of speech (See page 27.)

Clauses: Groups of words with their own subject and verb; some clauses can stand alone (independent) and some can't (dependent) (See page 29.)

Modification: One or more words that give other parts of the sentence more specific meaning (See page 42.)

Punctuation: "Road signs" or marks, such as the semicolon, the comma, and parentheses, used in writing to separate sentences and elements and to clarify meaning (See page 55.)

Parallelism: Using elements in sentences that are grammatically similar or identical in structure, sound, and meaning (See page 73.)

CHAPTER 1: The Foundation

As with anything you do, you need to start with the basics. After all, you wouldn't start putting furniture inside a house that hasn't been built yet, would you? Of course not! You would start with the raw materials. Nouns, pronouns, and verbs are the basics found within all sentences.

Nouns

Nouns are one of the main building blocks of a sentence. Nouns are the names of people, places, things, or ideas. A noun lets the reader know what or who you are talking about, even before you get to the action.

There are four different types of nouns:
1. common nouns
2. proper nouns
3. collective nouns
4. pronouns

Common nouns name **any** general person, place, thing, or idea.
Examples: *boy, girl, school, store, job, state, river*

Proper nouns name a **particular** person, place, thing, or idea.
Examples: *George, Susan, New York, Atlantic Ocean, Eiffel Tower*

Collective nouns name a **group** of people, places, or things. (See page 16.)
Examples: *crowd, herd, team, audience, band, family, town, company*

Pronouns take the place of specific nouns. Pronouns can be pesky, so we will learn more about them on page 12.
Examples: *I, you, he, she, it, we, they, me, you, him, her, us, them*

key: To tell if a word (other than a name) is a noun, place the word *the* or *a* before a word. If it makes sense—bam—you have a noun.
Examples: *The car, a bike, the mountain, a dog*

When to Capitalize Nouns

Names of specific people: *Leslie, Jamie, the Binghams*

Days of the week, months, and holidays but NOT seasons: *Sunday, May, Veteran's Day, Memorial Day, summer, autumn, fall, winter, spring*

Ranks and titles but only when used with a person's name: *Aunt Asha, General Washington, Dr. Weiss*

Geographic areas (cities, states, countries, counties, rivers, oceans, streets, parks, etc.): *Alabama, Mt. Washington, Foothill Lane, Rutland, Yellowstone National Park*

Regions of the United States: *the Midwest, the North, the South, the Southwest*

Historical periods: *The Industrial Revolution, the Revolutionary War, the Enlightenment*

Religions, nationalities, races of people, languages, and countries: *Muslims, Asians, African Americans, Hebrew, England, Irish stew*

The various names of sacred books: *the Bible, the Koran*

Specific school courses but not general subjects: *Algebra 101, History of the Middle East; I am taking algebra and history.*

Letters that stand alone: *T-shirt, X-ray, B+*

Titles of movies, books, magazines, chapters, articles, and songs: *It's a Wonderful Life, Little Women, National Geographic, "Backpacking through Vermont," "How to Cook Chicken," "The Itsy Bitsy Spider"*

Note: Longer works (books, magazines, albums) are italicized when typed and underlined when handwritten; shorter works (chapters, songs) are put in quotation marks and not italicized/underlined.

Pronouns

Pronouns are words that take the place of specific nouns. So, instead of saying:

Bobby ate cake. Bobby got sick, and Bobby couldn't go to school.

You could say:

Bobby ate cake. He got sick, and he couldn't go to school.

In the sentence above, the pronoun *he* takes the place of the noun *Bobby*.

There are several types of pronouns:

Personal pronouns refer to people, places, things, and ideas: *I, me, you, he, she, him, her, they, them, we, us, it.*

I threw the ball to you, and they threw the ball to us.

Possessive pronouns show ownership of something: *my, mine, your, yours, his, her, hers, its, our, ours, their, theirs, whose.*

The red backpack is yours, the blue one is his, and the green one is mine.

Reflexive pronouns (also known as intensive pronouns) refer back to the subject: *myself, yourself, himself, herself, itself, ourselves, yourselves, themselves.*

The student carried all her books into the classroom by herself.

They relied upon themselves to finish the coloring project.

Will she remember to help herself to the doughnuts on the desk?

Demonstrative pronouns point out a specific person, place, or thing without naming it: *this, that, these, those.*

This is interesting.

These are confusing.

Are those for us?

That is a great point!

Relative pronouns relate a group of words to a noun or other pronoun: *who, whoever, whom, whomever, which, that, where, wherever, when, whenever.*

The student who won is in my class.

The guinea pig that is brown is the cutest.

The pen, which is on my desk, works well.

Interrogative pronouns introduce questions: *what, which, who, whom, whose.*

Whose bicycle is this?

Which of these is the correct answer, Paula?

Whom did you ask to babysit your daughter while you were at the gym?

Indefinite pronouns do not refer to a specific person, place, or thing. *Another, both, everyone, most, no one,* and *several* are a few indefinite pronouns. (See page 16.)

A pronoun must take the place of one—and only one—specific noun! **The noun the pronoun refers to is called the antecedent.**

The teacher took pride in helping her students.

The pronoun *her* refers back to *teacher*, the subject of the sentence. *The teacher* is the pronoun's antecedent, the word that the pronoun refers back to in the sentence. Usually in our writing, the antecedent comes before the pronoun in the sentence.

 # Construction Zone

Pronouns are little words that often like to be bad. A pronoun can be like a pesky fly that ends up at the wrong place at the wrong time and annoys the wrong number of people.

If you can't tell what noun the pronoun is taking the place of = **bad thing**

If the pronoun does not agree with the noun = **another bad thing**

If the pronoun does not agree with the subject = **yet another bad thing**

The book has lost its cover. (singular noun/subject and pronoun)

The teachers know their students well. (plural noun/subject and pronoun)

Adding vague pronouns is a very easy mistake to make in your writing. Always check pronouns twice and make sure they are correct! Make sure to especially double check *it*. *It* is the peskiest pronoun within our writing!

*We were walking through the park, and **it** sounded great.* = **bad**

Who or what is the *it* referring to?

Pronoun Cases

Depending on the noun it is substituting in for, a pronoun will be one of three **cases:**

- **Nominative:** The subject
- **Objective:** The thing being acted upon
- **Possessive:** Showing ownership

Pronoun Cases						
Nominative	I	We	You	He/She/It	They	Who
Objective	Me	Us	You	Him/Her/It	Them	Whom
Possessive	My/Mine	Our/Ours	Your/Yours	His/Her/Hers/Its	Their/Theirs	Whose

Memorize the above chart. There are three general rules that help you figure out the correct pronoun case.

Rule 1 : Cross off the noun.

When more than one person is mentioned, cross off the other person and see if the sentence makes sense. Use your ear!

He asked my brother and me/I to go.
He asked ~~my brother and~~ me to go. **Correct!**
He asked ~~my brother and~~ I to go. **Incorrect**

Peter and me/I are going to the movies.
~~Peter and~~ me are (am) going to the movies. **Incorrect**
~~Peter and~~ I are (am) going to the movies. **Correct!**

When did you last write an e-mail to Anne and he/him?
When did you last write an e-mail to ~~Anne and~~ he? **Incorrect**
When did you last write an e-mail to ~~Anne and~~ him? **Correct!**

Rule 2 : Finish off the comparison.

There are two ways to understand Rule 2. You can either memorize that any comparison ending in a pronoun takes the nominative form, or—even better—when a comparison is implied and ends with a pronoun, finish off the comparison to hear the error. Use your ear!

Maria had more experience than she/her.
Maria had more experience than she (had experience). **Correct!**
Maria had more experience than her (had experience). **Incorrect**

Lindsey can eat as much as me/myself/I.
Lindsey can eat as much as me (can eat). **Incorrect**
Lindsey can eat as much as myself (can eat). **Incorrect**
Lindsey can eat as much as I (can eat). **Correct!**

Rule 3 : Prepositions always take the objective case.

Prepositions are those little words that indicate position (*of*, *for*, *to*). You can't use your ear on this one, so you must memorize this rule.

The card is for him/he.
Objective case: *him*
The card is for him.

The bug was on me/I.
Objective case: *me*
The bug was on me.

Brent is between you and me/I.
Objective case: *me*
Brent is between you and me.

key: It is easy to hear the mistake for most prepositional comparisons: *to me, for me, from me,* etc. The tricky one is *between*. *Between* always takes the objective case. It's always *between you and me,* NOT *between you and I.*

Collective Nouns

Collective nouns take the singular pronoun *it*. Be especially careful in your writing when using the pronouns *they* and *it*. Collective nouns can trick you!

Some nouns, like *team* or *family*, suggest a lot of people without being plural! Collective nouns can tempt you, but don't fall for their trap! These are nouns that are singular but collectively include multiple items. You'll want to refer to these nouns as *they*, but collective nouns are singular and need to take the pronoun *it*.

The team (collective noun) *was supposed to compete Friday but it had to forfeit.*

The school (collective noun) *posted its rules outside the main office.*

Some Common Collective Nouns				
team	committee	company	board	group
species	crowd	band	city	town
state	country	family	audience	class

Indefinite Pronouns: The "Special" Pronouns

The pronouns discussed all stand in for a noun in the sentence, or they emphasize a noun within the sentence. However, some pronouns like to keep you guessing. **Indefinite pronouns** do not name the words they replace, yet they function as nouns. Ready for a headache? Some indefinite pronouns are always singular, some are always plural, and some may be either singular or plural!

Anybody can see that the teacher is absent. (singular)

No one was home. (singular)

Somebody should pick up the ball. (singular)

Several of us want to go to the movies. (plural)

Both of my friends play an instrument. (plural)

Indefinite pronouns can be pretty pesky because they make sentences SOUND like the subject and verb do not agree, even if they do. When you see an indefinite pronoun, don't rely on the verb "sounding right" inside your head. Just follow the rules! There are exceptions, but these exceptions are rare.

Neither the tennis ball nor the net is in good condition.

OR

Neither the tennis ball nor the net are in good condition.

Neither is a singular pronoun and takes the singular verb *is*. Therefore, the first sentence is correct.

Either the DVD or the CD makes a terrific gift.

OR

Either the DVD or the CD make a terrific gift.

Either is a singular pronoun and takes the singular verb *makes*. Once again, the first sentence is correct.

Indefinite Pronouns: Singular vs. Plural Verbs		
Singular	**Plural**	**Singular or Plural**
each	both	none
either	few	any
neither	many	some
everyone	several	all
every		
everybody		
anyone		
no one		
nobody		

key: *Each, either,* and *neither* are ALWAYS singular. These words are tricky!

Verbs

Ready. Set. Go! **Verbs** provide the action. If the noun is the first building block of a sentence, then the verb is definitely the second building block. Without the almighty verb, you would be stuck describing a single scene instead of telling an action-packed story. Verbs create excitement by giving the subject (the noun) something to do.

There are two types of MAIN verbs:

1. **Action verbs** tell what the subject is doing. This is the action of the sentence. Example: *He jumps.* (*He* = subject; *jumps* = action verb)

2. **Linking verbs** express a state of being and do not show action. A linking verb links the subject to another word that describes this subject. Common linking verbs include: *am, are, is, was,* and *were.*

Construction Zone

Sometimes linking verbs can be tricky! Words like *grow, look, became, appear, taste, smell,* and *remain* are also linking verbs. How can you tell if a verb is a linking verb or an action verb? Simple! A verb is a linking verb if you can substitute *am, is,* or *are* (or a form of one of those verbs) for it.

Their bird is a falcon. (verb = *is*)

The cookie smells delicious. (linking verb = *smells*; substitute *is* for *smells*, and it works: *The cookie is delicious.*)

The dog appears hungry. (linking verb = *appears*; substitute *is* to test that it's a linking verb: *The dog is hungry.* Yes! It works!)

key: A verb is a linking verb if you can substitute the verb *am, is,* or *are* for it.

To be (linking) verbs *(is, are, was, were, etc.)* don't create as much excitement or meaning as action verbs. If you have little things to say, use *to be* verbs, but if you have BIG things to say—interesting, complex, exciting ideas—then use BIGGER and BETTER verbs.

Joan is a great teacher. (dull)

Joan wowed the class with her booming voice. (exciting)

key: Eliminate *to be* verbs from your writing.

Hold on! There is a third type of verb! Think of this next verb as the friendly verb—the verb that lends a helping hand. This third type of verb is not strong like the action and linking verbs and cannot stand alone; instead, this type of verb can only HELP the main action or linking verb. Thus, the name.

3. **Helping verbs** come before the main verb. Helping verbs help state the action or show time. Together, the helping verb and the main verb are called the **compound verb** or **verb phrase.**

    Carlos will drive to the movies tomorrow. (will = helping verb; *drive* = main verb; *will drive* = compound verb)

    helping verb + main verb = verb phrase
    will + drive = will drive

    I do want that cheeseburger. (do = helping verb; *want* = main verb)

Helping Verbs		
did	do	does
been	being	be
may	might	must
would	will	
was	were	
can	could	
have	has	
am	are	is
shall	should	

key: *Be, have,* and *do* can be used as helping verbs or as linking verbs.

Verb Tenses

What good would all these verbs be if we didn't know when they were taking place? That's why the tense is so important—it indicates *the time* an action takes place. There are several **verb tenses.** The simplest are past, present, and future tense.

Past tense—*I did*
Present tense—*I do*
Future tense—*I will do*

Ironically, the more troublesome tenses are the "perfect" tenses: These are tenses that combine the past with the present, past with the past, or present with future.

They don't sound so perfect do they?

Past perfect—*I had done*
Present perfect—*I have done*
Future perfect—*I will have done* (this tense is rare in writing)

key: The perfect tense is formed by the appropriate tense of the verb *to have* + the past participle of the verb.

A participle is used to form verb tenses. In the above examples, the participle is *done*. Here are some more examples of participles:

By this afternoon, Jason will have <u>read</u> the book. (*read* is the participle)
Mary arrived after I had <u>eaten</u> dinner. (*eaten* is the participle)
My brother has <u>finished</u> his homework. (*finished* is the participle)

key: A participle can also function as an adjective.

To really confuse things more and make this all sound like a troublesome tongue twister, we have the progressive tenses: tenses, which indicate continuing action (present), a past action that was happening when another action occurred (past), or an ongoing or continuous action that will take place in the future (future).

Present progressive—*I am doing*
Past progressive—*I was doing*
Future progressive—*I will be doing*

 key: The present and past progressive tense is formed by using a helping verb (*am/is/are* or *was/were*) with the verb form ending in *-ing*.

Finally, let us finish this tongue twister by putting it all together:

Present perfect progressive—*I have been asking*
Past perfect progressive—*I had been asking*
Future perfect progressive—*I will have been asking* (rarely used)

Note: The present and past perfect progressive are formed by using the verb *to have* with the verb form ending in *-ing*.

This all sounds confusing, but don't let the twisters overwhelm you! A good writer memorizes a simple rule: Do not throw a bunch of actions together and let the reader fumble around with various tenses—present one minute, present perfect the next, etc. Instead, a good writer keeps the tense the same throughout the sentence, paragraph, or essay.

In your writing, pay attention to numbers and dates. Numbers and dates are CLUES to help you figure out which tense should be used within a sentence.

*Ten days from now, **I will** go to the store.* (future tense)
*Hopefully, in five months, **I will be doing** a job that I love.*
(future progressive tense)
*For three years, **I have been asking** for a new desk.* (present perfect progressive tense)

key: When writing about literature, ALWAYS use the present tense.

Irregular Verbs

Sometimes a form of a verb just isn't what you'd expect—this is why they're called **irregular verbs!** The best way to master these verbs is to memorize them. Use this handy chart of common irregular verbs.

Present Tense	Past Tense	Past Participle
arise	arose	arisen
bring	brought	brought
choose	chose	chosen
dive	dove or dived	dived
draw	drew	drawn
drink	drank	drunk
drive	drove	driven
eat	ate	eaten
fall	fell	fallen
fly	flew	flown
freeze	froze	frozen
give	gave	given
get	got	gotten
go	went	gone
grow	grew	grown
hang (thing)	hung	hung
hang (person)	hanged	hanged
know	knew	known
lay	laid	laid
lie	lay	lain
ride	rode	ridden
ring	rang	rung
rise	rose	risen
run	ran	run
see	saw	seen
shrink	shrank	shrunk
slay	slew	slain
speak	spoke	spoken
spring	sprang	sprung
steal	stole	stolen
swim	swam	swum
take	took	taken
tear	tore	torn
weave	wove	woven
write	wrote	written

Active and Passive Voice

Just like people, verbs have different personalities, and it's important to get to know these personalities before using them in your writing. Some verbs are bold **(active)** while others are quiet **(passive).**

A verb is in the active voice when the subject performs the action:

Sun-Hee won the contest.

A verb is in the passive voice when the subject receives the action:

The contest was won by Sun-Hee.

Both active and passive voices are grammatically correct, but active voice is direct and powerful.

Passive Voice—Whisper	Active Voice—Shout
Jim was hit by Jack.	*Jack hit Jim.*
The ball was hit by Tommy.	*Tommy hit the ball.*
The door was slammed by Lina.	*Lina slammed the door.*

Notice in the above examples that the passive voice is longer and usually contains *by*.

key: Write in active voice. *By* often indicates passive voice within a sentence.

Moody Verbs

Verbs don't just have personalities; they have moods, too! A verb's mood indicates the writer's attitude toward what he or she is saying, so it's important to pay close attention to mood in your own writing. After all, you wouldn't want to give the impression that you hate having fun, playing games, or going on summer vacation, would you? Here are the different moods your verbs can convey.

Indicative: States facts: *I gave everyone lollipops.*

Imperative: Gives commands and instructions: *Give everyone lollipops.*

Interrogative: Asks a question: *Should I give everyone lollipops?*

Conditional: Indicates a conditional state that will cause something else to happen: *I would give everyone lollipops if I had lollipops to give.* (*Might, could,* and *would* indicate the conditional mood.)

Subjunctive: Expresses wishes and conditions that are contrary to fact (something that is not really true): *If I were president, I would give out free lollipops to everyone!*

When a Verb Is Not a Verb

Sometimes, verbs don't act like verbs. They throw the rules out the window and start to act like nouns, adjectives, or adverbs. These rebel verbs are called either gerunds or infinitives.

A **gerund** is a verb ending in *-ing* and used as a noun.

> *I enjoy selling.* (direct object)
> *Selling requires special skills.* (subject)
> *She is experienced in selling.* (object of preposition)

An **infinitive** is a verb introduced by *to* and can be used as a noun, an adjective, or an adverb.

> *To do her a favor is a pleasure.* (noun/subject)
> *She asked to see the book.* (noun/object)
> *I still have two more contracts to draft.* (adjective/modifies *contracts*)
> *He resigned to take another position.* (adverb/modifies *resigned*)

An adjective (*draft*) modifies a noun or adjective and an adverb (*take*) modifies a verb. See pages 34–37 to learn more about adjectives and adverbs.

Here is a little trick to remember:

Gerunds = facts

> *Wayne enjoys <u>going</u> to concerts.*
> *We resumed <u>working</u> after our ice cream break.*
> *Maria appreciated <u>getting</u> help from Peter.*

Infinitives = intentions, desires, or expectations

> *Joey <u>expected to get</u> a good job after graduation.*
> *Last year, Sally <u>decided to become</u> an English major.*
> *The team has <u>agreed to go</u> back to the field.*

The above is a trick and not a steadfast rule because there are some exceptions. But usually the trick works! When trying to decide between an infinitive and a gerund, ask: "Is it an *intention* (infinitive) or is it a *fact* (gerund)?"

Here is a hard and fast rule, though: Always use a gerund (*-ing*)—not an infinitive (*to*)—directly following a preposition. (See page 24.)

> *This water is safe for <u>to drink.</u>* (incorrect)
> *This water is safe for <u>drinking</u>.* (correct)

key: Gerunds *(reading)* = facts
Infinitives *(to read)* = intentions

Subject/Predicate

You can't tell your story (or any story as a matter of fact) without the sturdy sentence. And to be able to create strong, effective sentences, you first need to understand the basics.

The foundation (base) of any sentence is a subject (noun) and a predicate (verb). All sentences must express a complete thought and need a **subject** and a **predicate** to do so.

The complete subject is the noun or pronoun that performs the action. It also contains all the words that help to identify the main person, place, thing, or idea in the sentence.

> *The popular baseball player decided not to play in today's game because of a sore arm.*

> *The uncooperative class did not want to complete the assignment.*

The **simple subject** is the main noun or pronoun that performs the action within the complete subject. The subject is the person, place, or thing the sentence is about.

> *The popular baseball player decided not to play in today's game because of a sore arm.*

> *The uncooperative class did not want to complete the assignment.*

 key: Asking the question "What?" or "Who?" will help identify the subject.

The **complete predicate** is the main verb (action) along with all of its modifiers. The complete predicate tells what the subject is or does.

> *I bought that jacket last week.*

> *DeAndre was reading the book when the phone rang.*

The **simple predicate** is just the verb in the sentence.

> *I bought that jacket last week.*

> *DeAndre was reading the book.*

key: Asking the question, "What did/does the subject (noun) do?" will help identify the verb.

CHAPTER 2:
Building a Great Sentence

Good sentences become great sentences by using descriptive words and phrases **(modifiers)** to create more detail in our writing. Which house would you choose to live in? A house with nothing but four walls and a roof or a castle complete with a moat, a drawbridge, turrets, mirrors, and a grand ballroom? The castle, of course! In this section, you will learn about the grammatical tools that will turn that plain house into an extraordinary castle; in other words, how to turn good writing into great writing!

Phrases

Phrases are very important in your writing because they add variety and description. A **phrase** is a group of words that functions as a part of speech and doesn't contain a subject and a verb. A phrase cannot stand alone. Phrases help your readers visualize the people, places, and things in your sentences.

Fearing an accident, Alberto drove slowly. (Fearing an accident is a phrase that modifies, or describes, *Alberto*.)

All of the students climbed on the bus. (*of the students* and *on the bus* are prepositional phrases; *of the students* modifies *All* and can be eliminated; *on the bus* modifies *climbed* and can be eliminated; *All... climbed* = subject/verb. See page 39 for more on prepositional phrases.)

White Cottage, our favorite ice cream spot, is off the beaten path. (*our favorite ice cream spot* is a phrase that serves as an interrupter; see page 54.)

Before recess was over, the kids played a game of kickball. (*Before recess was over* modifies and makes more descriptive the sentence, *The kids played a game of kickball.*)

Phrases add description to a sentence, giving more detail to your writing. You want to fortify your sentences by correctly using descriptive phrases; however, you also need to understand how to take away these phrases to find the foundation of the sentence—the simple subject and verb. See page 52 for more about reducing a sentence to its foundation (subject/verb).

key: Phrases DO NOT contain a subject and verb.

Verbal Phrases

A **verbal** is a verb (action word) used as another part of speech. There are three types of verbals: **participles, gerunds,** and **infinitives.** Each serves a different function in a sentence.

Participle phrases function as adjectives. These phrases include the participle and its related words. A participle is a present tense verb that often ends in -*ing*.

Walking home from school, Kayla met a friend. (Walking is the participle and modifies the noun *Kayla*. So *Walking home from school* is the participle phrase.)

Gerund phrases function as nouns. A gerund is a present tense verb that ends in -*ing*.

Jogging through the woods was a wonderful time for Nina and her friends. (In this sentence, *Jogging through the woods*, the gerund phrase, serves as the subject of the sentence. *Jogging* is the gerund.)

Infinitive phrases function as nouns, adjectives, or adverbs; however, they are usually used as nouns. An infinitive is a present tense verb and is usually preceded by *to*.

To finish this book by tonight will be very difficult. (In this sentence, *To finish this book*, an infinitive phrase, serves as the subject of the sentence. *To finish* is the infinitive.)

Clauses

A **clause** is a group of words that has both a subject and a verb. Basically, any simple sentence is a clause, but unlike sentences, not all clauses can stand alone. There are two types of clauses.

An **independent clause,** also known as a **simple sentence,** is a group of words that can stand alone as its own sentence.

Paulo was a student.

A **dependent clause,** also known as a **subordinate clause,** cannot stand alone. This clause needs to be accompanied by an independent clause to make sense. (Get it? The dependent clause depends on the independent clause!)

After he finished his chores

This dependent clause is not a sentence. To make sense, we need to add an independent clause like *Joe went to the store*. By combining them together, we get the following complete sentence:

Joe went to the store after he finished his chores.

The word *after* before *he finished his chores* takes away the sentence's ability to stand alone. Lots of words do this. The magical words that turn sentences into NOT (incomplete) sentences are called **subordinating conjunctions.** *Even though, now that, unless, because,* and *although* are just a few subordinating conjunctions. (See page 46 for a list of subordinating conjunctions and more about these words.)

Now watch the transformative magic, and see how subordinating conjunctions add detail and excitement to plain, boring sentences.

Darcell walked to school. → *Darcell walked to school <u>even though</u> it was raining.*

Carly will play soccer. → *Carly will play soccer <u>now that</u> her foot injury has healed.*

I'll be there. → *I'll be there <u>unless</u> my flight is delayed.*

They did not want dessert. → *<u>Because</u> they ate a big dinner, they did not want dessert.*

Jamie wore a rain jacket. → *<u>Although</u> it was sunny, Jamie wore a rain jacket.*

key: Clauses DO contain a subject and a verb.

Sentence fragments are "wannabe" sentences that can't stand alone! A fragment is a group of words that does not contain a complete thought and often lacks a subject or verb. Take a look at the following fragments:

Went home past the school

Because I wanted to go

And her sister

One word that turns a strong sentence into a "wannabe" is the word *because*. Strong writers do NOT begin a sentence with *because* UNLESS they want to attach this fragment (incomplete thought) to a sentence (complete thought).

Because I was hungry—NOT a complete thought

Because I was hungry, I ate dinner.—Complete thought

Aha! The word *because* is a magical word known as a subordinating conjunction. Like magic, *because* turns independent clauses (sentences) into dependent clauses! (See page 46 for more about subordinating conjunctions.)

If you find a fragment in your writing, connect the fragment to the main sentence by adding a comma.

On the way to school. I saw Amy and her brother. (bad)

On the way to school, I saw Amy and her brother. (good)

 key: DO NOT begin a sentence with *because* UNLESS it is connected to the main sentence with a comma.

Run-on sentences are two sentences (independent clauses) that are joined together without appropriate punctuation or a conjunction:

They were not dangerous, poisonous snakes they were nonvenomous. (bad)

They were not dangerous, poisonous snakes. They were nonvenomous. (good)

Essential and Non-Essential Clauses

Who, *which*, and *that* are three little words that create big problems in our writing!

Who refers to a person.

Which refers to a thing.

That refers to a thing.

But if both *which* and *that* refer to things, how do you tell the difference between them?

The answer is simple. Follow this one rule to figure out which word to use:

If information CAN be eliminated from the sentence and the sentence still makes sense, use *which*. If the information CAN'T be eliminated from the sentence because the sentence will no longer make sense or the main message will change, use *that*.

> *My blue sweater, which costs $25, has two pockets in the front.*

Here, the non-essential clause, *which costs $25*, can be removed, and we still have a complete sentence: *My blue sweater has two pockets in the front.*

> *We hung the sign above the front door, which was painted bright red.*

Which was painted bright red is the non-essential clause that can be removed, still leaving us with a complete sentence.

> *That black jacket is my new favorite.*

In this sentence, *That black jacket* cannot be removed because then we would be left with *is my new favorite*—definitely not a complete sentence.

 key: **Which** cannot stand alone! It must have a comma or preposition before it. **That** should stand alone! DO NOT put a comma before it.

Who can be used as both an essential and a non-essential clause. If the *who* clause is necessary to retain the meaning of the sentence, then there shouldn't be commas placed around it; if the *who* clause does not present essential information and does not affect the main sentence if omitted, then place commas around it.

My sister, who is the oldest child in our family, loves to ski.

The non-essential clause, *who is the oldest child in our family*, can be removed: *My sister loves to ski.*

Jackie knows who the winner is.

The essential clause, *who the winner is*, cannot be removed from the sentence without removing essential information.

Construction Zone

Remember, *which* clauses are non-essential. Therefore, don't use too many of them in your writing. One is fine, but look what happens when your writing is overloaded with non-essential clauses:

I rode the school bus, which was really old, to the track meet, which was an hour away. When I got to the track meet I talked to my coach, who was wearing a blue sweatshirt, about what races I was going to race that day, which was cold and rainy.

If they are overdone, *which* clauses distract the reader and diminish your message.

Who vs. _whom_ is confusing! Adding an "m" to the end of _who_ creates some big problems, and the difference between the two words can get pretty confusing. However, looking at how the word is used in a sentence is a great place to start.

The word **_who_** is used when talking about the **subject**, and the word **_whom_** is used as **a direct object** or an **object of a preposition.** (A direct object is the noun that receives the action from the subject.)

Who followed the dog? (_Who_ is the subject.)

The girl who followed the dog lives down the street. (_Who_ modifies the subject.)

Whom did you see at the gym? (_Whom_ modifies the verb _see_.)

With whom did you get a ride? (_Whom_ follows a preposition.)

Still confused? Try the following trick. When you're trying to decide whether to use _who_ or _whom_, ask yourself if the answer should be _he_ or _him_. Both _him_ and _whom_ end in "_m_," so it's easy to remember that if you can answer the question with _him_, use _whom_ in the question!

Who/whom do you play basketball with?

The answer to the question would be _I play basketball with him_, not _I play basketball with he_, so you know _whom_ must be in the question.

Who/whom played basketball?

The answer to the question would be _He played basketball_, not _Him played basketball_, so you know _who_ must be in the question.

 key: If you can't remember whether to use **_whom_** or **_who_**, remember that **_him_ = _whom_** and **_he_ = _who_.**

Adjectives

Tired of plain, boring sentences? Well, then, it's time to use adjectives!

Adjectives are words that modify—describe, quantify, or identify—a noun or pronoun. The purpose of adjectives is to give more information so that the writer's meaning is clear. For example, what would happen if you went to the store and said, "I want the shoes"? Is this an interesting, clear sentence? No! Do we know what type of shoe you want? No! Use adjectives to describe the shoes you want and to make your message interesting and clear.

> **Basic sentence:** *I want the shoes.*
>
> **Better sentence:** *I want the purple shoes.*
>
> **WOW sentence:** *I want two pairs of the shiny, high-heeled purple shoes in a size eight.*

Now we know the color, style, size, and number of shoes you want!

Choose the right adjective! Consider the adjectives *hungry, angry,* and *stuffed* in the following sentences. Then decide which sentence you would most like to hear as you walk through the woods.

> *There is a <u>hungry</u> bear behind you.*
>
> *There is an <u>angry, hungry</u> bear behind you.*
>
> *There is a <u>stuffed</u> bear behind you.*

The last one, right? In these sentences, those little descriptive words can make a huge difference. *Hungry, angry,* and *stuffed* all describe the noun *bear,* and all of these descriptions give you some very important pieces of information. A comma is used to separate adjectives.

Attaching Adjectives to Linking Verbs

Sometimes adjectives come **after** linking verbs. (See page 18 to learn more about linking verbs.) Whenever this happens, the adjective describes the subject of the sentence.

Astrid's favorite shirt is <u>yellow</u> and <u>blue.</u>

Is is the linking verb. The adjectives *yellow* and *blue* describe the subject of the sentence—the *shirt*. The linking verb *is* links the adjectives with the subject.

The afternoon appears dark because of the clouds in the sky.

The adjective *dark* describes the subject of the sentence—the noun *afternoon*. The linking verb *appears* links the adjective with the subject.

As discussed in the section on verbs (pages 18–25), you can tell if a verb is a linking verb if it can be replaced with *am*, *is*, or *are*.

The afternoon <u>is</u> dark. (*Appears* is a linking verb because it can be substituted with *is*.)

key: To find the subject of the sentence, ask the question *What?* Whatever receives the action of the sentence is the subject.

Changing Nouns to Adjectives

Here is an important trick: By adding a suffix, you can change some nouns into adjectives. For example, the noun *poison* is changed to the adjective *poisonous* when you add the suffix *-ous*. Other common suffixes that can change nouns into adjectives are *-ly*, *-ic*, *-like*, *-ish*, and *-al*.

friend—friendly
life—lifelike
athlete—athletic
sheep—sheepish
universe—universal

Adverbs

Just as adjectives describe nouns to make writing more interesting, **adverbs** are used to modify verbs, adjectives, or another adverb. They describe how, when, and to what extent the action (verb) took place.

> **How:** *We did our homework underlined carefully.*
> **When:** *They often play cards together.*
> **To what extent:** *He really likes to play tennis.*

Let's look at how adverbs can transform boring sentences into exciting ones.

> *I ran during the game.* = boring

This sentence doesn't tell us too much about what happened, does it? Were you fast? Were you slow? Were you even running in the right direction?

> *I ran rapidly and repeatedly during the game.* = exciting

Now readers know that they will not be able to keep up with you!

The following examples show how adverbs (the underlined words) can be used to add detail to different parts of speech.

> **Adverb modifying an adjective:** *The painting is very beautiful.*

> **Adverb modifying a verb:** *I quickly ran to the store.*

> **Adverb modifying another adverb:** *The kite was flying surprisingly high.*

---

key: Adverbs are loveLY! Many adverbs (not all) end in *-ly: carefully, suspiciously, loudly.*

Construction Zone

Be on the lookout for verbs that have to do with **senses**—feel, look, sound, taste, and smell—because sometimes they function as linking verbs, but other times they function as action verbs!

I feel <u>bad</u> for my friend.

OR

I feel <u>badly</u> for my friend.

In the above example, *I feel <u>bad</u>* is correct because you are talking about your own state of mind and therefore need an adjective for description. *Bad* relates to you and to the pronoun *I*.

I feel badly would mean you are having difficulty in feeling at all! No feeling in your fingers! What a terrible thing! *Badly* relates to the verb *feel*, which is not what you are trying to describe.

In general, the verb *to feel* will take an adjective *(happy, sad, good, bad, angry, relieved)* after it to indicate your feelings.

I feel <u>bad</u> about having said that.

OR

I feel <u>badly</u> about having said that.

Are you trying to say your fingers have a problem touching things? No! You are describing your state of mind, so the adjective form is used: *I feel <u>bad</u> about having said that.*

I smell <u>bad.</u>

Go take a shower! *Bad* is describing *I* (the pronoun).

I smell badly.

You can't smell the delicious dinner cooking in the oven. *Badly* describes *smell* (the verb).

Good vs. *Well*

Unfortunately, verbs of senses are not the only ones confusing adjectives and adverbs. To add some more confusion into the mix, let's take a look at **good** and **well** and how *well* functions BOTH as an adverb and as an adjective.

1. ***Good*** is always an **adjective.**

   You did a good job on the report.

   You are a good friend.

2. ***Well*** is an **adjective** used to describe good health.

   I feel well.

   You look well after being out sick all week.

   (*Look* and *feel* are verbs of senses. *Well* is describing *you*, a pronoun.)

3. ***Well*** is an **adverb** when it's used for anything else.

   You write well.

   I hear well. [You can *hear* (verb) the teacher talking in the front of the classroom.]

Prepositions and Prepositional Phrases

A preposition shows the relationship of a noun or pronoun to another word in the sentence. Most prepositions are small words, but they play a big role in making a boring sentence into something quite lively. Like hot peppers, prepositions really spice up your writing. They express the where, when, and relationship between words within a sentence.

The best way to identify prepositions is to memorize the list of some of the most common prepositions.

Common Prepositions	
about	into
above	like
across	near
after	of*
against	off
along	on
among	onto
around	opposite
at	outside
before	over
behind	past
below	through
beneath	to*
beside	toward
between	under
beyond	underneath
by	until
down	up
for*	upon
from	with
in	within
inside	without

*key: The prepositions *of*, *for*, and *to* are three of the most frequent words in English.

Here's a good trick to help you memorize the words on the previous page. Think of the word *box*—*in* a box, *around* a box, *through* a box, *from* a box. Most prepositions are words that give direction to a box. Therefore, if you are having a hard time memorizing your prepositions, just memorize the few prepositions that DO NOT relate to a box, such as *to*, *for*, and *of*.

key: A trick for recognizing a preposition is to see if it relates to the word *box*—*in* a box, *on* a box, *along* a box, etc.

Prepositions introduce **prepositional phrases.** A prepositional phrase is made up of a preposition, a noun, and all the words between the preposition and noun.

> *I bought the flowers for my mother.*

Here, *for my mother* is the prepositional phrase that modifies the basic sentence *I bought the flowers*. It is made up of the preposition *for* and ends with the noun *mother*.

> *Sarah keeps her schoolbooks beneath her bed.*

In this case, *beneath her bed* is the prepositional phrase because it is made up of the preposition *beneath* and ends with the noun *bed*.

Watch how prepositions and prepositional phrases make dull sentences more exciting:

Blah sentence: *I went to bed.*

WOW sentence: *After I hiked twenty miles, I went to bed inside my old tent, under the starry sky.*

Blah sentence: *Heather scored a goal.*

WOW sentence: *After running every day and paying close attention to her coach, Heather finally scored a goal with the ball flying above the goalie's arms.*

Interjections

Yippee! **Interjections** add spice and emotion to our writing. These one- or two-word expressions electrify our sentences: *Zap! Yikes! Zowie! Pow!*

An interjection is a word or group of words that is used as an exclamation to express emotion. These words are usually included at the beginning of a sentence and are used to exclaim, protest, or command. Also, some interjections express sounds. An interjection does not need to be followed by an exclamation point, but it often is. If the interjection does not express strong emotion, then a comma should be used.

<u>Nah,</u> I didn't finish my homework.

<u>Oh,</u> you didn't tell me that we are going fishing.

<u>Yay!</u> I won!

<u>Wow!</u> You look terrific in that outfit.

<u>Snap!</u> The book was shut in my face.

<u>Mmmm,</u> the hamburger is delicious.

Introductory phrases such as *yes*, *no*, *hello*, and *goodbye* can also be classified as interjections.

<u>Yes,</u> I am going to the dance.

<u>Hello!</u> How was your trip?

Interjections do not always have to come at the beginning of a sentence; they can also be found in the middle and at the end of a sentence.

You find this reading difficult, <u>huh</u>?

When I think about that dog—<u>my goodness</u>—he is so cute!

key: Interjections are rarely used in formal or academic writing.

Modification

Adjectives, adverbs, phrases, and clauses add sparkle to lackluster sentences and brighten up our writing, making it more specific and interesting.

A **modifier** is a word or phrase that provides more information within a sentence.

Modifying words, clauses, and phrases at the beginning, middle, and end of simple sentences create variety and add diversity to your writing. These modifiers change unimaginative and featureless simple sentences (only containing a subject and predicate) into detailed and descriptive examples of writing.

While Ellen was cleaning her room, the bike was stolen. (adverbial clause)

After his car was totaled beyond repair, Archie knew that he'd have to buy a new one. (prepositional phrase)

Digging deeper, the reporter asked probing questions and hunted for more sources. (gerund phrases)

Beginning and Ending Sentences with *-ing*

Sentences that begin or end with *-ing* (gerund phrases) make for great writing. With a little *-ing*, snoozing sentences turn into lively, complex, and interesting ones! By using sentences that begin with an *-ing* word, a skilled writer will change his or her writing, making it much more sophisticated and keeping the interest of the reader.

Sleepy sentence: *I went to school.*
Lively sentence: *Wanting to learn, I went to school, even though there was six feet of snow outside.*

Sleepy sentence: *Cody went for a run.*
Lively sentence: *Looking out the window, Cody saw a clear blue sky, realized it wasn't going to rain, and went for a run.*

Sleepy sentence: *Kate saw her grandparents.*
Lively sentence: *Last Friday afternoon, Kate saw her grandparents and spent more than three hours talking and visiting.*

Construction Zone

A **dangling** or **misplaced modifier** is an introductory phrase or clause at the beginning of a sentence that is misplaced because the word it modifies is not actually in the sentence or is too far away from the word it is intended to modify.

> *Because she was hungry, the pizza looked amazingly good to Sarah.*

OR

> *Because she was hungry, Sarah thought the pizza looked amazingly good.*

At first, both sentences look correct. Realize, though, that *because she was hungry* is not a sentence! It's an adverbial clause trying to grab onto the real main sentence. In order to provide something to grab hold of, you must provide a noun or pronoun to which the modifier (adverbial clause in the above sentence) can be attached. Therefore, ask the question, *Who is hungry?* Sarah is, NOT the pizza! Sarah is the subject; hence, the second sentence is correct.

> *Unhappy, the match was forfeited by the tennis player.*

Is the match unhappy or is the tennis player unhappy? I hope the tennis player! The sentence needs to read: *Unhappy, the tennis player forfeited the match.* (correct)

> *Chilled to the bone, the hot soup tasted good to the skiers.*

The hot soup is not chilled to the bone, but the skiers are! The sentence needs to read: *Chilled to the bone, the skiers thought the soup tasted good.*

There can be a misplaced modifier in the middle of a sentence.

Modifiers can dangle, but they can also be improperly placed within the sentence. Every modifier (phrase, clause, word) must have a noun or pronoun that it clearly modifies. Misplaced modifiers create confusing, and often funny, sentences. To correct misplaced modifiers, move the modifier (person or thing that's part of the action) closer to the word or phrase it is supposed to modify.

– continued

Max found his lost keys walking across the street in front of his apartment.
What? The keys walk? Unless we live in a magical world, keys do not walk! Therefore, the sentence needs to read: *Walking across the street, Max found his lost keys.* Now we are back in reality, and Max is doing the walking, not the keys!

There can be a misplaced modifier at the end of a sentence. We are not done yet! Modification problems can also occur at the end of a sentence. Clauses or phrases that come at the end of the sentence must properly modify the object within the sentence. In this case, the object of the modifier must be found directly BEFORE the comma.

She gave the sweater to her mother, which was soft and blue.
Soft and *blue* refers to the sweater, not the mother. Therefore, the sentence needs to read: *She gave her mother a sweater, which was soft and blue. Soft and blue* modifies *sweater.* So now it's clear that the sweater is blue, and her mother is not!

Conjunctions

Now it's time to put all those exciting phrases, clauses, and sentences together! **Conjunctions** are words that connect other words or groups of words and show how they are related.

Coordinating Conjunctions

Coordinating conjunctions are those little words that connect phrases, clauses, and sentences. It is important to remember that whatever is found on one side of a conjunction must be found on the other.

To remember the coordinating conjunctions, just memorize the acronym **FANBOYS** *(for, and, nor, but, or, yet, so)*.

It is important to create **parallel structure** using coordinating conjunctions. Coordinating conjunctions help create the parallel sentences that make your writing smooth and balanced. Let's use the conjunction *and* to show how a FANBOY serves as an equal sign between two balanced phrases, clauses, or sentences.

She liked to watch TV, and she liked reading.

OR

She liked to watch TV, and she liked to read.

The second sentence is correct: *to watch* AND *to read*. Nice and equal. Here are some other examples:

Infinitive phrase to infinitive phrase: *She is deciding whether to finish her book or to go for a run.* (See page 28.)

Active voice to active voice: *Sonal hit the ball, and Jim caught the ball.* (See page 23.)

Noun to noun: *I like ketchup and mustard on my hot dog.*

Independent clause (sentence) to independent clause (sentence): *Megan was hungry, but she didn't want to eat before dinner.*

Notice the fourth sentence has a comma before the conjunction. ALWAYS place a comma before the conjunction when you are connecting two independent clauses (sentences).

Andy wanted a new car, but he couldn't afford the insurance.
The kids complained about the heat, yet they still went to an outdoor camp every day of the week.

However, don't use a comma when you are NOT connecting two sentences together.

He is neither tall <u>nor</u> dark haired.

On Monday night, we went out for ice cream <u>and</u> to the movies.

Subordinate Conjunctions

Not all sentences are composed solely of equal parts. Usually there are some parts that are essential to the main idea and some others that serve to support or give additional information about the main idea. **Subordinate conjunctions** are used to help connect parts of a sentence that are unequal. The subordinate conjunctions below help connect "inferior" subordinate clauses to the main sentence.

Common Subordinate Conjunctions		
after	if only	till
although	in order that	unless
as	now that	until
as if	once	when
as long as	rather than	whenever
as though	since	where
because	so that	whereas
before	than	wherever
even if	that	while
even though		

Sam can go to the concert, <u>unless</u> it's on Friday night.

<u>Since</u> yesterday was my birthday, I got the extra piece of cake.

<u>Because</u> you studied pre-algebra, you can take algebra.

 key: *Subordination* means lower ranking, inferior, lesser. This will help you remember that a subordinating conjunction is used to connect the "inferior" phrase or clause to the main sentence.

Conjunctive Adverbs as Transitional Phrases

Adverbs are very versatile tools in your grammar toolbox because they strengthen your writing in a number of ways. **Conjunctive adverbs** are adverbs that work as **transitional phrases,** connecting your sentences and joining similar ideas within your writing.

Conjunctive Adverbs That Serve as Transitional Phrases	
accordingly	in the first place
at the same time	indeed
besides	likewise
consequently	moreover
for example	nevertheless
for this reason	on the contrary
furthermore	on the other hand
hence	still
however	therefore
in addition	thus

Conjunctive adverbs have a dual role. They connect independent clauses (i.e, sentences), and they also illustrate the relationship between the two sentences. Sentences joined by conjunctive adverbs must be separated by a semicolon. Also, the conjunctive adverb must be separated from the beginning of the sentence with a comma.

The medicine tasted bad; <u>however</u>, it made me feel better.

I did not study; <u>consequently</u>, I failed the quiz.

<u>Nevertheless</u>, I promise to study the next time.

Conjunctive adverbs can also be used in the middle of a sentence. However, these adverbs need to be blanketed in commas in order to be used correctly within the sentence.

Jamal, <u>still</u> wet from swim practice, went to the store five minutes before it closed.

Leslie brought four dresses, <u>in addition</u> to the one she was wearing, so that she would have all her favorite clothes with her on vacation.

I am not convinced, <u>however</u>, that you are telling the truth.

Correlative Conjunctions (Hand Holders)

When constructing a balanced sentence, some things have to go hand in hand to create parallel structure.

Correlative conjunctions are **hand holders**. All you need to know is that you can't break the buddy system for the following:

Not only... but also

Not... but

Neither... nor

Either... or

Both... and

Whether... or

Whenever you see one of the above in a sentence, make sure to find its partner!

The senator was pleased <u>not only</u> with voter turnout, <u>but also</u> with voter support of her proposal.

It is <u>not</u> that I don't want to go, <u>but</u> that my mother will not let me go.

<u>Neither</u> Frank <u>nor</u> Rameena arrived to work on time.

Sara was going to order <u>either</u> the steak <u>or</u> the salmon.

<u>Both</u> Leah <u>and</u> her sister were at the play.

<u>Whether</u> he goes <u>or</u> he stays, I don't care.

Comparisons

Sentences must compare two things that are alike. This is the apples-to-oranges rule: Apples must be compared to apples and oranges to oranges. In a well-written sentence, properly used **comparisons** create strong, clear, parallel sentences.

Than and *As*

Make sure your comparisons make sense! You want to compare shoes to shoes, money to money, etc. Sometimes, a comparison is not obvious. If the comparison is positioned at the end of the sentence and is implied, finish the sentence to make sure your comparison is parallel. Simply think of a crane and pick up the noun on the left side of the comparison, and move it to the right side!

The judges felt that Brian's cake tasted better than Joe. (bad)

In this sentence, a cake is incorrectly compared to a person. This is difficult to hear at first, but, if you finish the sentence, the mistake becomes obvious.

The judges felt that <u>Brian's cake tasted better than Joe's cake.</u> (good)

Reports show that a sales representative's salary is higher than a doctor. (bad)

This sounds OK at first, but again, finish off the sentence to ensure a parallel comparison.

Reports show that <u>a sales representative's salary is higher than a doctor's salary.</u> (good)

 key: *Than* and *as* need to make equal comparisons. Think of a crane picking up the noun on the left side of the comparison and moving it to the right side!

Like

Like is almost never correct in your writing. The only time that *like* is acceptable is when you are comparing two unlike things (*My love is like an endless road*) and when you are using *like* as a preposition.

<u>Like</u> *you, I always read before I go to bed.* (preposition)

My anger is <u>like</u> a blazing fire. (comparison of two unlike things)

Big, Bigger, Best

Most comparisons are made by using different forms of adjectives or adverbs. The degree of comparison is indicated by the ending (usually -*er* and -*est*) or by the use of *more* and *most* (or *less* and *least*).

Adjectives and adverbs can show degrees of quality or amount with the endings -*er* and -*est* or with the words *more* and *most* or *less* and *least*. Most modifiers have three forms: **positive, comparative,** and **superlative.**

The **positive** form is the dictionary form. It describes without comparing.

a big book   *spoke forcefully*

The **comparative** form compares the thing modified with one other thing.

a bigger book   *spoke more* (or *less*) *forcefully*

The **superlative** form compares the thing modified with two or more other things.

the biggest book   *spoke most* (or *least*) *forcefully*

Degrees of Some Irregular Adjectives and Adverbs		
Positive	**Comparative**	**Superlative**
good	better	best
bad	worse	worst
little	less	least
some	more	most

Four Types of Sentences

Now we are ready to take a simple sentence and turn it into something extraordinary!

There are **four types of sentences:**

1. Simple
2. Compound
3. Complex
4. Compound-complex

A **simple sentence** has a subject and verb:

I ran.

A **compound sentence** is constructed by sticking two simple sentences together with a conjunction *(and, but, or, nor, for, so, yet)*:

I ran and I fell.

A **complex sentence** has a phrase or clause attached to the simple sentence:

Because I was late for class, I ran.

A **compound-complex sentence** has a phrase or clause attached to a compound sentence:

Because I was late for class, I ran and I fell.

Strong writing revolves around enhancing the main structure: the simple sentence. Using varied sentence structure throughout your writing will make it engaging and exciting. You don't want to lull your reader to sleep by using the same sentence structure again and again throughout your writing. Mix things up! Jazz up sentences with modifiers and prepositional phrases. Use conjunctions to connect simple sentences and build balanced sentences with lots of meaning. But don't overdo it! Remember to use some shorter simple sentences in your writing as well. Variety is the key to keeping your reader engaged.

Subject/Verb Agreement

When you work with a friend on a project and if you agree with one another, things go smoothly. If you do not agree, your project will be a mess! We don't want our sentences to be a mess, so we have to make sure our subjects and verbs agree with each other. If the subject is singular, the verb must be singular. If the subject is plural, the verb must be plural. The easiest way to check subject/verb agreement is to take a sentence down to its foundation!

Follow these three steps to check subject/verb agreement:

1. First, **identify the subject**. In a simple sentence, this is easy:
   George walked to school. (*George* is the subject.)

But, in a more complex sentence it can be tricky to identify the subject. So you will have to strip down the sentence to its most basic form.
   The books on the shelf in the library needs dusting.

There are a lot of nouns in the sentence. Which one is the subject? *Books? Shelf? Library?*

To figure it out, we need to eliminate the extras. Ask the question *What?* or *Who? What needs dusting? Books!*

The books just happen to be on the shelf in the library, but that doesn't really matter. *On the shelf in the library* includes extra phrases we don't need.

Stripped down to the (basic) sentence: *The books <u>needs</u> dusting.*

2. Next, **determine if the subject is singular or plural:** *Books* is plural, so the verb must also be plural.

3. Finally, **make the verb agree with the subject:** *The books <u>need</u> dusting* is correct. Now, you can put the sentence back together:

Corrected sentence: *The books on the shelf in the library <u>need</u> dusting.*

Here are some more examples of the three steps for checking subject/verb agreement.

Sentence: *Scott and Allison, hoping to win the lottery, buys tickets each week.*
Stripped (basic sentence): *Scott and Allison, ~~hoping to win the lottery~~, buys tickets.*
Corrected: *Scott and Allison <u>buy</u> tickets each week.*

Sentence: *The kids, while playing in the park, starts a game of tag.*
Stripped (basic sentence): *The kids, ~~while playing in the park~~, starts a game of tag.*
Corrected: *The kids <u>start</u> a game of tag.*

Recap: The steps for checking subject/verb agreement are:

1. Find the subject of the sentence by eliminating the extras (prepositional phrases, interrupting phrases, beginning or concluding phrases).

   a. **Cross out prepositional phrases:** *The bird in the yard began chirping.*

   b. **Cross out interrupting phrases:** *The team, ignoring tradition, will update the uniforms.*

   c. **Cross out non-essentials (phrases, dependent clauses, adjectives, and adverbs):** *Early this morning, Emma awoke to finish studying for her difficult exam.*

2. Determine whether the subject is singular or plural. Remember that collective nouns, nouns referring to a group as a whole *(team, audience, wolf pack)*, are singular!

3. Make the verb agree with the subject. Singular subjects are paired with singular verbs; plural subjects are paired with plural verbs.

key: Plural or singular? Think *he* for singular nouns and *they* for plural so that you can easily hear subject-verb errors: *He walks/They walk.*

 # Construction Zone □□□

Tricky Situations for Subject/Verb Agreement

Inverted word order: When the subject and verb are inverted (the verb comes before the subject), it can be hard to check if they agree.

There were two books on the shelf. (*were*—the verb—is placed before *two books*—the subject.)

Also, notice that the sentence begins with *There were. There* often indicates inverted word order, so pay attention to *There is, There are, There was, There were, There has,* and *There have.*

key: *There* at the beginning of a sentence is a warning that the verb comes before the subject.

– continued

Collective nouns: Although collective nouns suggest a lot of people or things, they are NOT plural! These are nouns that are singular but collectively include multiple items.

The audience in the auditorium is cheering. (The collective noun *audience* and the verb *is* are both singular.)

See page 16 for more information about collective nouns.

Interrupting phrases: Interrupting phrases are often found between two commas or two dashes. Therefore, you can follow a general rule: Cross out anything sandwiched (found) between commas.

Indefinite pronouns: Indefinite pronouns do not name the words they replace, yet they function as nouns. Some indefinite pronouns are always singular, some are always plural, and some may be either singular or plural. See page 16 for more information about indefinite pronouns.

Punctuation

Punctuation is the nuts and bolts of writing because it holds sentences together.

Commas

Commas are like road signs. They give you direction, tell you where to pause, and make information clear. There are several comma rules to understand, so make sure you and the rules are buddy-buddy.

The "Comma *and/or/but*" Rule

This is a tricky but simple rule. The "comma *and*," "comma *or*," and "comma *but*" rules are all the same. If you have a conjunction *(for, and, nor, but, or, yet, so)* separating two complete sentences, then you need to place a comma before the conjunction. Put simply: "comma *and*" = complete sentence, period. **If you don't have a complete sentence on both sides of the conjunction, no comma is required.**

Sentence: *Michelle, and her boyfriend Esteban went rafting.*

Think: *Michelle. Her boyfriend Esteban went rafting.* (Incorrect—not two complete sentences)

Corrected: *Michelle and her boyfriend Esteban went rafting.*

Sentence: *The leaves on the trees are starting to turn colors, and the nights are getting longer and longer.*

Think: *The leaves on the trees are starting to turn colors. The nights are getting longer and longer.* (Correct! This compound sentence contains two sentences (independent clauses) joined by the conjunction *and*. Therefore, a comma plus *and* is needed.)

Sentence: *You can attend a concert, or you can go with me to the zoo.*

Think: *Or* separates two sentences (independent clauses). *You can attend a concert. You can go with me to the zoo.* (Correct! Therefore, a comma plus *or* is needed.)

Single Comma Rule

You don't want random commas inserted all over the place. There are specific instances that require a single comma. What do all of the rules below have in common? One comma is used to indicate where the reader should naturally, logically pause. See that? You need to pause between *naturally* and *logically* in the preceding sentence! Generally, the one-comma rule applies to introductory phrases and elements.

Use a comma after words such as *well, yes, no, why,* etc. when any of these words begin a sentence.

> *Well, I think I will go take a walk.*
>
> *Yes, I would like more carrots.*

Use a comma to set off a question from the rest of the sentence or to indicate when you're directly addressing someone.

> *It's true, isn't it?*
>
> *Is that you, Steve?*

Use a comma after a prepositional phrase or phrases that come at the beginning of a sentence.

> *Near the gate at the end of the lane, I watched the wild stallion race out of the corral.*
>
> *In paintings by modern artists, colors are very bright.*

Use a comma after an introductory adverbial clause—clauses that begin with such words as *when, after, while, because, since,* etc. (See page 42.)

> *After Miguel performed in <u>the play, he</u> gave a huge bow to the audience.*
>
> *Because we quickly found the source of the <u>fire, everyone</u> went home safe.*

A comma is used when writing a date, to separate the day of the month and the year.

> *I am going on July 10, 2015.*

A comma is used to separate the name of a street from a city and also the name of a city from the name of the state or country.

> *I live at 150 Foothill Lane, Northport, New York.*

The Listing Comma Rule

Any list requires commas between the listed items. These items can be gerunds, nouns, adjectives*, infinitives, phrases, adverbs, or verbs.

Please bring to the picnic milk, bread, eggs, and cheese. (nouns)

The big, brown, fuzzy bear was adorable. (adjectives)

Opening the door, yelling in excitement, and laughing at each other, we came back to class after a long recess. (gerund phrases)

Charlie slowly, carefully, and precisely finished his school project. (adverbs)

We decided to eat, to drink, and to clean up before watching a movie. (infinitives)

Covered in chocolate, layered with hot fudge, and served with ice cream, this piece of cake was sure to be incredible. (participle phrase)

*key: Do not put a comma between an adjective and a noun that form a pair: *disc jockey, pop star, cookie jar, cell phone.*

The Comma Sandwich Rule

Two commas are used to surround, or sandwich, clauses, phrases, and words that are not essential to the sentence's meaning. If you remove the words "sandwiched" between the two commas, you need to be left with a complete sentence. To clarify, "a sandwich" (although a delicious, descriptive addition to the sentence) is not essential to understanding the main purpose of the sentence.

Here are some clues to help you decide whether the sentence element (sandwich) is essential. If you answer *yes* to any of these questions, then the element is non-essential and should be sandwiched between two commas.

- If you leave out the clause, phrase, or word, does the sentence still make sense?

- If you move the element to a different position in the sentence, does the sentence still make sense?

- Does the clause, phrase, or word interrupt the flow of words in the original sentence?

  Kyra, <u>who likes animals</u>, wants to be a veterinarian. (clause)

  He tossed his homework aside and pulled his pie, <u>topped with a melting scoop of vanilla ice cream,</u> toward him. (phrase)

  She spoke at length, <u>perhaps,</u> because she was nervous. (word)

Construction Zone

The following are some comma no-nos.

1. A comma alone cannot separate two complete sentences. The separation of two sentences by a comma only is incorrect. **This rule has no exceptions.**

  Mark loves cheese, Blanca hates it. (incorrect)
  Mark loves cheese. Blanca hates it. (correct)

When a comma is incorrectly used to separate two complete sentences, it creates a run-on sentence. See page 30 for more information about the nasty run-on sentence.

– continued

There will be a lot of rain this afternoon, wear your raincoat to school.
(incorrect—this sentence is a run-on; because the comma separates two independent clauses, there needs to be either a conjunction, semicolon, or a period)

There will be a lot of rain this afternoon. Wear your raincoat to school.
(correct)

There will be a lot of rain this afternoon, so wear your raincoat to school.
(correct)

2. Prepositional phrases do not always have to get sandwiched between two commas. If it is a brief phrase (fewer than five words) and NOT at the beginning of the sentence, then the phrase does not need to be sandwiched between commas. Remember, a prepositional phrase is a non-essential. (See page 39.) If it is already removable, you don't need to use punctuation that says "remove me," as two commas do.

3. Essential clauses CANNOT be removed from a sentence. Sometimes a sandwich is an illusion (not as it appears). Look at the following sentence:

   A great girl, Michelle went to the store, hoping to get ice cream.

   If you eliminated *Michelle went to the store* because it is sandwiched between commas, you are left with *A great girl hoping to get ice cream.* What? This makes NO sense!

   Michelle went to the store. = sentence (essential clause)

   A great girl = an adjective phrase

   hoping to get ice cream = gerund phrase (direct object of *went*)

   Therefore, the two phrases (one at the beginning and one at the end) create a sandwich illusion!

4. DO NOT put a comma between an adjective and a noun that form a pair: *black cat, wide receiver, small car.*

The Semicolon—Let's Be Equal!

Sometimes sentences are buddy-buddy; they are close sentences that like to hang out together. In these cases, you want to use a friendly **semicolon** rather than a strict period. Semicolons act like a period, separating two sentences (independent clauses) as well as a coordinating conjunction *(for, and, nor, boy, or, yet, so)*. However, they are more than periods; they are "friendly" because semicolons indicate a close relationship between the two sentences.*

> *The hour is over; it is time to put your pencils down and stop working.*

> *All mammals have hair on their bodies; all reptiles are cold-blooded.*

Semicolons are also used to join two sentences that are connected by a conjunctive adverb *(however, nevertheless, therefore, moreover, for example,* and *consequently)*.

> *Feeding the birds is a good idea; however, don't spill the birdseed all over the garage.*

> *I am going for a walk now; nevertheless, I will still go for a run with you later.*

Please note that an additional, rare rule that applies to semicolon usage is not discussed in this section.

A semicolon must have a complete sentence on both sides.

The Apostrophe

Apostrophes do not have to turn into catastrophes if you know how to use them properly! Think of apostrophes as signposts at the end of your words. They help your reader follow the road of your writing by indicating both to whom an object belongs and when there is a combination of two words.

Possession Rules

Apostrophes are used to show ownership when coupled with an *s*. Apostrophe-*s* rules can get confusing, so be careful.

First, ask yourself if anything owns anything else. If not, then no apostrophe is needed. However, if possession is being indicated, then you need an apostrophe. **Generally, *'s* is translated into *owns something*.**

Rule 1 : An apostrophe plus *s* (*'s*) is used for singular nouns:

Mike owns the bike = Mike's bike

The dog owns the collar = The dog's collar

Rule 2 : Just an apostrophe (') is used if the plural noun ends in an *s*:

The doctors own the office = The doctors' office

The bicycles have many broken wheels = The bicycles' broken wheels

Rule 3 : An apostrophe plus *s* (*'s*) is used for plural nouns that do not end with an *s*:

The women's book club meets this Thursday.

The children's school is open this week.

Rule 4 : If a name ends in an *s*, the possessive is formed without the additional *s*:*

Ross' cookies taste great.

My boss' keys are on the desk.

Construction Zone

*Technically, you can write *Ross's* or *boss's*, but the better rule is to just add an apostrophe without the *s* to avoid a tongue twister!

Belonging to **and** *of* **Phrases**

key: A useful trick to help you determine an apostrophe's placement is to change the possessive phrase into *belonging to* or into an *of* phrase to discover the basic noun.

Keats' poem ➔ *the poem* <u>*belonging to*</u> *Keats* = possessive is *Keats'*

In two hours' time ➔ *In the time* <u>*of*</u> *two hours* = *Hours* is base; possessive is *hours'* and not *hour's*

The family's boat ➔ *The boat* <u>*belongs*</u> *to the family* = *Family* is the owner, so apostrophe is in the right spot

Construction Zone

The familys' boat ➔ *The boat* <u>*belongs to*</u> *the familys*. Does this make sense? No. *Familys* is not a word. *Families* needs to be the base. The correct usage is *The families' boat*, meaning MANY families own the boat.

The Contraction Rule

Contractions involve two words smushed together, with some of the letters pulled out. Talking fast? Want an informal tone in your writing? Want your writing to sound as if you are talking directly to the reader? The basic rule for forming a contraction is to insert an apostrophe in the space where the letters have been omitted.

Common Contractions		
I	am	I'm
you	are	you're
he	is	he's
we	are	we're

It's Important to Know the *Its* Rules!

It's = It is

Its = ownership/possession

<u>It's</u> easy (notice how I am using the word as a contraction) to confuse a possessive pronoun *its* with the contraction *it's*.

Hold On! There Are Two Other Uses of the Apostrophe

1. Use the apostrophe to form the **plural of a lowercase letter** by placing an *'s* after the letter: *Alec used two <u>b's</u> in his sentence.*

2. Use an apostrophe to **show where the letter or letters are left out in a word or number:** *He graduated in <u>'05</u>.*

The Colon Rules

Colons are used to indicate that a definition, explanation, or list is to follow. Colons may or may not separate two complete sentences. In general, colons are used for the following: (See how I am using the colon? The explanation is coming!)

1. To indicate a **definition**

    Perspicacity: wisdom.

2. To indicate a **list**

    I had to buy several things at the grocery store: milk, eggs, cheese, and bread.

3. To indicate an **explanation**

    I have been working since I was 16: I needed to pay for college and wanted to start saving early.

The Dash Rules

Dashes for the most part act like commas or parentheses and are used to "sandwich" interrupting phrases. However, unlike commas and parentheses, dashes add power and force to your writing. Anything between two dashes is non-essential, meaning the word or phrase can be eliminated and the sentence still makes sense. Often, the dash is used instead of the comma because the writer wants to summarize or highlight a word or series of words within a sentence.

> *When we arrived at the restaurant—one of our favorites—we had to wait more than two hours before we were seated.*

> *The sight of Niagara Falls—especially when seen for the first time—is breathtaking.*

A dash is also used to indicate a sudden break in the sentence.

> *Fruits, protein, and vegetables—these are all food groups we need.*
>
> *Everyone believed the news story—even my uncle, the most cynical among us.*

key: The dash is considered more forceful than the comma.

Parentheses

Parentheses enclose material that is of minor or secondary importance in a sentence—material that supports, clarifies, comments on, or illustrates what precedes or follows it.

> *I thought I had memorized the biology textbook. (Boy, was I wrong!)*

> *We must always try to be honest with each other. (But are we even sure what honesty really is?)*

> *For a long time (too long, as far as I'm concerned), not all people were taught how to read and write.*

Parentheses are also used to enclose numbers:

> *His first year at the school (2012) was a difficult one.*
>
> *The summer Manny was born (1990) was exceptionally hot.*

Construction Zone

Be careful with your use of punctuation with parentheses. Punctuation that refers to the material enclosed in parentheses occurs inside the marks while punctuation belonging to the rest of the sentence comes outside the parentheses. If a complete sentence is found within the parentheses, then you must include a period, exclamation point, or question mark.

My mom told me we are going into the city tomorrow (how exciting!), so I need to remember to wear my new sweater.

Next weekend we are going to visit my uncle (who I haven't seen in four years).

Ellipses

Ellipses (three little dots) might look like a bunch of periods (…), but they do not function like a period. Unlike a period, an ellipsis doesn't end! Instead of indicating the end of a sentence, these three dots indicate omitted material or long pauses, and experienced writers use them to show that a section of writing is not complete.

Ellipses indicate that you have deleted words from a passage you are quoting:

"We the people of the United States… establish this Constitution for the United States of America." (The Preamble to the United States Constitution)

Ellipses also show a pause or interruption in your writing:

I only vaguely remember what we did on Thanksgiving 10 years ago… I think we visited my grandmother in New York.

CHAPTER 3:
Finishing Touches

It is the finishing touches that make a house into a warm, inviting home. You can live in a big, fancy house, but if you do not make the home clean, inviting, and friendly, nobody will want to visit. Good writing is the same way. It should be uncluttered, clear, and exciting. Writers want to choose their words carefully in order to create a message or picture that others can understand, enjoy, and learn from… words readers want to visit!

Wordiness

Pick the stronger (better) sentence:

Redundancy, repeating repetitive words over and over and over again, is a resounding no-no-no in writing.

OR

Redundancy is a huge no-no in our writing!

Hopefully, you picked the second one. Sometimes it is better to be short and sweet rather than long and boring.

Be clear! Be concise! No, this does not mean that you eliminate description, images, and words that add to the beauty of the language. Such words enhance the meaning of your writing. However, get rid of the empty words, words that fill up your writing, fog your meaning, and clutter your message. Here are three steps to clearer and bolder writing:

1. **Eliminate unneeded words and phrases.**

   Wordy: *These types of reading problems are really quite difficult to solve.*
   Better: *Reading problems are difficult to solve.*

   Wordy: *Reading has a value from the view of an educational standpoint.*
   Better: *Reading has a value from an educational standpoint.*

   Wordy: *The gas supply was sufficient enough for the drive home.*
   Better: *The gas supply was sufficient for the drive home.*
   Best: *We had enough gas to drive home.*

2. **Combine sentences that repeat information.**

Wordy: *If the mountain is covered in pine trees, it must be forested. And if there is a forest, there are probably pine trees that animals hide in.*

Better: *The mountain was pine-covered and forested—animals hid easily.*

Wordy: <u>*Harry Potter and the Sorcerer's Stone*</u> *is a best-seller. It was written by J. K. Rowling.* <u>*Harry Potter and the Sorcerer's Stone*</u> *is a fantasy novel.*

Better: <u>*Harry Potter and the Sorcerer's Stone*</u> *by J. K. Rowling is a best-selling fantasy novel.*

3. **Make passive sentences active.**

Wordy: *The car was given to me by my grandfather.*

Better: *My grandfather gave me the car.*

Wordy: *The sandwiches were eaten by us.*

Better: *We ate the sandwiches.*

4. **Eliminate inverted word order *(there is/there are, there was/there were, there has/there have)*.** Inverted word order refers to a sentence that places the verb before the subject. Although this sentence construction can provide sentence variety, inverted word order often waters down your message. (See page 53 for more information on word order.)

Wordy: *There were two books on the shelf.* (*were*—the verb—is placed before *two books*—the subject)

Better: *Two books were on the shelf.*

Wordy: *There are four lunch plans that students can choose.*

Better: *Students can choose from four lunch plans.*

Best: *Four lunch plans are offered.*

5. **Use strong, active verbs.** *To be or not to be?* Definitely NOT *to be!* Be verbs *(is, are, was, were, been)* often result in wordiness and water down your writing. Also, make sure to write in the active voice whenever possible. (See page 23.)

Wordy: *A high-fat, high-cholesterol diet is bad for your heart.*

Better: *A high-fat, high-cholesterol diet harms your heart.*

Wordy: *Riding on the roller coaster is frightening to Geri.*

Better: *Riding on the roller coaster frightens Geri.*

 key: Shortest is sweetest at times. Vary your sentence structure.

20 Redundant Phrases	
Wordy	**Concise**
at all times	always
at that point in time	then
at the present time	now
complete stop	stop
due to the fact that	because
for the purpose of	for
if and when	if
in order to	to
in spite of the fact that	although
in the event that	if
in view of the fact	since
is an example of	is
more often than not	often most
not different	similar
not include	omit
small in size	small
will be able to	can
will have to	must
with reference to	regarding
with the exception of	except

 key: Eliminate *to be* verbs from your writing.

Diction

Diction refers to the words you use in your writing, and choosing between certain pairs of words can get downright confusing! *Accept* or *except? Bring* or *take?* If you keep track of the meanings and memorize the explanations below, you can avoid misusing words in your writing.

Accept: (verb) to receive willingly
Will you accept this reward for doing the extra credit assignment?

Except: (preposition) but; other than
All of the kids except Dina used blue notebooks.

Adverse: (adjective) opposed; unfavorable
Because of the adverse weather conditions, school was closed for the day.

Averse: (adjective) not willing or inclined; reluctant
Amy was averse to cheating because she knew it was wrong.

Affect: (verb) to influence
The teacher's absence will affect the daily lesson plan.

Effect: (noun) result; (verb) to cause to become; to accomplish; to produce
The effects of the tutoring session will raise the student's grade. (noun)
The newly added science class will effect change in the schedule. (verb)

Already: (adverb) by this time
Can we get in the car already?

All ready: (adjective) completely prepared
Are you all ready for the audition tonight?

Among: (preposition) refers to more than two people, places, things, or ideas
The teacher distributed the snacks among the 20 children.

Between: (preposition) refers to two people, places, things, or ideas
Joey and I divided the sandwich between the two of us.

Beside: (preposition) by or at the side of; alongside; next to
Alani sat beside her friend Jesse at the school assembly today.

Besides: (preposition) in addition to; as well as; (adverb) furthermore
Besides reading a chapter in a book, Jake also has to finish five math problems. (preposition)
Besides, I don't want to go tonight. (adverb)

Bring: (verb) to move something to a place
    Remember to <u>bring</u> your notebook to class each day.

Take: (verb) to move something away from a place
    After lunch, please <u>take</u> your trash off of your desk and throw it away.

Can: (verb) to know how to; to be able to
    I know I <u>can</u> get a perfect score on the next vocabulary quiz.

May: (verb) to be allowed to
    <u>May</u> I go outside for recess after I finish these five problems?

Cite: (verb) to quote or mention
    Make sure to <u>cite</u> any articles you use in your argument, so people will know where your information is from.

Site: (noun) piece of land; location
    The school plans to build a new playground on that <u>site</u>.

Farther: (adjective and adverb) used to designate a physical distance
    She could hit a tennis ball <u>farther</u> than anyone else in her lesson group.

Further: (adjective and adverb) additional
    After finishing the workbook, the kids waited for <u>further</u> instructions from their teacher.

Fewer: (adjective) countable, individual things
    Emily had <u>fewer</u> pencils than Lauren.

Less: (adjective) use with uncountable amounts and volumes.
    After soccer practice, there was <u>less</u> water in Jane's water bottle than there was in Beena's.

Formally: (adverb) in accordance with the rules
    I am going to announce <u>formally</u> that I am running for class president.

Formerly: (adverb) previously
    I was <u>formerly</u> a model in Italy.

Lay: (verb) to put or set something down; when discussing things, use the word *lay*
    I <u>lay</u> down the book.

Lie: (verb) to rest in a horizontal position; when discussing people, use the word *lie*
    I am going to <u>lie</u> down and read my book.

Loose: (adjective) not tight
His loose clothing made him look smaller than he really was.

Lose: (verb) misplace; not win
I hate to lose my keys.

Sit: (verb) to stay seated
Please sit down!

Set: (verb) to put in place
Please set the books on the table.

Than: (conjunction) word used to compare two or more people, places, things, or ideas
I would rather do my science homework than do my Spanish homework.

Then: (adverb) at that time or soon after/next
I went to the game and then to the gym.

There: (pronoun and adverb) describes a location or a physical or abstract place
There is a big bear in my backyard. (adverb)
Where is it? It is there. (pronoun)

Their: (pronoun and adjective) shows possession
Their dirty clothes were in the car.

They're: a contraction for *they are*
They're going to the zoo.

To: (preposition) (infinitive) used to indicate what someone/something moves toward; used to indicate the place where someone participates in a certain activity; used to indicate the direction of something
He went to school. (preposition)
We don't need to buy that now. (infinitive)

Too: more than enough; synonym for also
Sally was too tired to go to school.

Two: (adjective) number
Two students were walking down the hall.

Construction Zone

Here are some tips on using these words correctly!

Due to: Use *due to* only if you mean *caused by* or *resulting from*. Do not use *due to* if you can substitute *because of* or *on account of*. Hint: If a sentence begins with *due to*, it's probably wrong, like this one: *Due to inclement weather, school was canceled*.

Hardly/scarcely: Double negatives! Do not use *hardly* with a negative verb as in: *She can't hardly see without her glasses*. *Hardly* is already a negative word, and you don't need two of them.

> *The store had scarcely no milk.* (incorrect)
>
> *The store had no milk.* (correct)

Of vs. have: Do not use *of* as a verb! *Might of* is never correct. *Might have*, *Will have*, and *Would have* are correct. *Of* sounds correct as a verb because of the contraction forms: *might've*, *would've*, *could've*, etc. Don't be fooled, though!

> *If I write this essay tonight, I will of finished my homework for the rest of the week.* (incorrect)
>
> *If I write this essay tonight, I will have finished my homework for the rest of the week.* (correct)
>
> *I could of gone to the game.* (incorrect)
>
> *I could have gone to the game.* (correct)

Where: ONLY use this word to express direction and location.

> *Where are you going?* (correct)
>
> *I live in a house where it is 200 years old.* (incorrect)

While: This word is usually used to indicate time. Writers should replace *while* with *although*, *but*, and *or* for everything else.

> *The student stared at the computer monitor while he listened to the teacher.* (correct)
>
> *While the results are encouraging, future research still needs to be performed.* (incorrect)
> (*While* should be replaced with *Although* because time is not being addressed.)

key: *where* = direction

Parallelism

Sentences that are correctly and effectively written are sentences that are balanced. A balanced sentence is one in which related actions, ideas, and descriptions are presented in the same form.

Notice the above sentence and how it utilizes parallel structure: *Sentences that... are sentences that...* This is parallelism!

> **key:** Parallel structure is not only grammatically correct, but it also makes our sentences POP!

If you save a penny, it is just as if you have earned it.
OR
A penny saved is a penny earned. (Oh...so much better! This sentence is POPPING!)

Examples of parallel structure:

Jim and Cory visited New York City. (noun to noun; also subject parallel with subject)

Roya went to Cleveland and to Chicago. (prepositional phrase to prepositional phrase)

Jim and Cory visited New York City, and Roya went to Cleveland and Chicago. (independent clause equal to independent clause, or—keep it simple—sentence parallel to sentence)

Creating a Rhythm

You may use parallelism for a series of words, phrases, or clauses. These sentences create a flow in your writing.

Our flag is red, white, and blue. (parallel words)

Kadeem ran up the steps; Susan ran down the steps; Joe stood bewildered on the landing. (parallel clauses)

"...of the people, by the people, for the people..." is stated in the Gettysburg Address. (parallel phrases)

Construction Zone

Warning! Do not try to make nonparallel things parallel!

Jerry was a reader, a writer, a studier, and neat. (bad)

Jerry was a reader, a writer, and a studier. He was also neat. (better)

Also, do not overuse parallelism. If you do, your writing becomes tiresome and repetitive. Emphasizing everything is the same as emphasizing nothing!

Transitions

Coherence and flow are two crucial elements to writing. Ideas should be linked with transitional words and sentences: *in essence, with this in mind, undeniably, in short,* etc. Transitions glue our ideas together—sentence to sentence and paragraph to paragraph.

Transitional Words and Phrases

Continuation/Addition: *again, also, as well as, besides, coupled with, furthermore, in addition, likewise, moreover, nevertheless, similarly*

Consequence: *accordingly, as a result, consequently, for this purpose, for this reason, hence, otherwise, so then, subsequently, therefore, thereupon, thus, wherefore*

Contrast/Comparison: *by the same token, contrast, conversely, in contrast, likewise, on one hand, on the contrary, on the other hand, similarly*

Reversal of Thought: *although, but, despite, however, instead, rather, though, yet*

Emphasis: *above all, chiefly, especially, particularly, singularly*

Exception: *aside from, besides, except, excepting, excluding, other than, outside of*

Highlighting: *chiefly, especially, for instance, including, in particular, namely, particularly, specifically, such as*

Generalizing: *as a rule, as usual, for the most part, generally, generally speaking, ordinarily, usually*

Illustration: *as an example, as an illustration, for example, for instance, for one thing, illustrated with, in this case*

Similarity: *comparatively, correspondingly, coupled with, identically, likewise, moreover, similar, similarly, together with*

Restatement: *in brief, in essence, in other words, in short, namely, that is, that is to say, to put it differently*

Sequence: *afterward, at first, at the same time, earlier, first of all, for now, for the time being, in conclusion, in the first place, in time, in turn, later, later on, meanwhile, next, simultaneously, soon, then, the next step, to begin with, with this in mind*

Summarizing: *after all, all in all, all things considered, briefly, finally, in any case, in any event, in brief, in conclusion, in short, in summary, in the final analysis, in the long run, on the whole, to summarize, to sum up*

Beginnings: *at first, at the beginning, early on, first, first of all, initially, in the beginning, in the first place, the first, to begin, to start*

 key: Remember reversal-of-thought transitions with *BIRTHDAY*—*b*ut, *i*nstead, *r*ather, *th*ough, *h*owever, *d*espite, *a*lthough, *y*et.

Idioms

Idioms are language quirks—grammatically correct for no grammatical reason! In a sense, an idiom is a rule of usage that applies only to a particular instance. Idioms include all of the expressions that are unique to English, including clichés like *pain in the neck*, *jumping the gun*, *raining cats and dogs*, etc. Some of the most common errors occur with preposition usage. Sadly, you simply need to memorize and know what preposition to supply in certain instances. Below is a list of some of the most common idioms with prepositions. Idiom problems are the hardest things to catch in our writing. Make sure to look for them before you hand in your essays!

Common Idioms with Prepositions	
Unidiomatic (incorrect)	**Idiomatic (correct)**
according with	according to
authority about	authority on
capable to	capable of
comply to	comply with
conform in	conform to (or with)
consists in	consists of
die from	die of
different than	different from
ever now and then	every now and then
equally as bad	equally bad
excepting for	except for
familiarity of	familiarity with
felt as if	felt as though
happy at	happy with
in accordance to	in accordance with
incapable to do	incapable of doing
in search for	in search of
independent from	independent of
intend on doing	intend to do
in the year of 2015	in the year 2015

Common Idioms with Prepositions	
Unidiomatic (incorrect)	**Idiomatic (correct)**
long ways off	long way off
off of	off
on account of	because
on a whole	on the whole
over with	over
plan on	plan to
prior than	prior to
proponent of	proponent for
preoccupied in	preoccupied with
seldom or ever	seldom if ever
similar with	similar to
superior than	superior to
try and see	try to see
type of a	type of
working at	working with

Nuts and Bolts Grammar Reference Guide

Here is a collection of many of the important grammar tips provided throughout this book, all in one convenient place.

- To tell if a word (other than a name) is a noun, place the word *the* or *a/an* before the word.

- Use *it* sparingly in your writing.

- A verb is a linking verb if you can substitute the verb *is* or *was* for it.

- Eliminate *to be* verbs from your writing.

- When writing about literature, ALWAYS use the present tense.

- *By* often indicates passive voice.

- Write in the active voice.

- Asking the question *What?* or *Who?* will help identify the subject.

- Asking the question *What did/does the subject (noun) do?* will help identify the verb.

- *Which* CANNOT stand alone! It must have a comma or preposition before it.

- *That* SHOULD stand alone! DO NOT put a comma before it.

- *Him = whom* and *he = who.*

- Adverbs are loveLY! Many adverbs (not all) end in *-ly.*

- Trick for recognizing many prepositions—think of the word *box: <u>in</u> a box, <u>on</u> a box, <u>along</u> a box*, etc.

- *Than* and *as* need to make equal comparisons. Think of a crane picking up the noun on the left side of the comparison and moving it to the right side!

- Plural or singular? Think *he* for singular nouns and *they* for plural so that you can easily hear subject-verb errors: *He walks/They walk.*

- The apostrophe always goes at the end of the word that is doing the "owning." If the tree house belongs to one boy, it is *boy's tree house;* if the tree house belongs to many boys, it is *boys' tree house.*

- The dash is considered more forceful than the comma.

- Shortest is often sweetest in your writing.

- Vary your sentence structure/length.

- *Where* = direction and *when* = time.

- Remember *BIRTHDAY* for reversal-of-thought transitions: *but*, *instead*, *rather*, *though*, *however*, *despite*, *although*, *yet*.

- Check all dates and time periods to make sure tense is correct.

- *It's* = *it is*; *its* = possessive.

- Think of FANBOYS—for, and, nor, but, or, yet, so—when creating a parallel sentence. These words help serve as an equal sign between two balanced phrases, clauses, or sentences.

- A balanced sentence is one in which related actions, ideas, and descriptions are presented in the same form. When a sentence does this, it utilizes parallel structure.

Parts of Speech Review

Directions: Identify each underlined word as a part of speech, and write your answer on the line before the sentence (n = noun; pro = pronoun; adj = adjective; v = verb; advb = adverb; prep = preposition; c = conjunction; and int = interjection).

1) _____ The kids watched the <u>programs</u> before going to bed.

2) _____ Mike <u>programs</u> his DVR so that he doesn't miss his favorite TV shows.

3) _____ The girl made a wish and threw a penny into the <u>well.</u>

4) _____ I feel <u>well.</u>

5) _____ <u>Yes!</u> Our vacation next week will be so much fun!

6) _____ <u>They</u> have been going to the same school for the past two years.

7) _____ Luke always tried to get to class <u>quickly</u> so he could talk to the teacher before the rest of the students got there.

8) _____ My brother bought <u>red</u> wheels for his skateboard.

9) _____ The students wanted to go outside after lunch, <u>so</u> the teacher took them to the park.

10) _____ The students organized a community service trip over <u>their</u> spring vacation week.

11) _____ In order to make the school garden, everyone had to help move the <u>dirt.</u>

12) _____ The girl <u>had to leave</u> the party early in order to catch the last train home.

13) _____ The <u>leaf blower</u> is outside the garage.

14) _____ <u>Fun!</u> I can't wait to come to your party on Saturday.

— Parts of Speech Review continued

15) _____ The cleverly edited commercial tricked my younger brother <u>into</u> thinking that babies could skillfully rollerblade.

16) _____ The couple made a <u>down payment</u> on their new apartment.

17) _____ The soccer captain told Melanie to <u>pass</u> the ball.

18) _____ <u>Ouch!</u> I just burned my tongue taking a sip of hot coffee.

19) _____ <u>Each</u> athlete on the team visited hospitalized children during the off-season.

20) _____ After the school handed out new materials, Kate's <u>backpack</u> was very heavy.

21) _____ The new driver foolishly <u>increased</u> his speed, hoping to get to a station before he ran out of gas.

22) _____ Leila and Sally were identical twins, <u>but</u> they spoke differently.

23) _____ The boy and <u>his</u> mother walked together.

24) _____ She relied <u>on</u> her phone and her alarm clock as well as her messaging center.

25) _____ <u>Oh,</u> pardon me. I wasn't looking where I was going.

Collective Nouns

Directions: Circle the collective noun and then pick the proper pronoun and/or verb form in the underlined portions of each sentence.

1) A species, in order to prosper, must be endowed with some means of distributing their/its individuals over an ever-increasing territory.

2) Any analysis of Italian music would demonstrate the extent to which the musical heritage of that country is preserved in its/their music.

3) The deer has become such a pest in residential areas that it may become necessary to limit their/its population.

4) While the country had been plagued by language divisions that had sometimes created internal discord, they were/it was finally enjoying a feeling of national pride.

5) Although the band was popular and rich beyond belief, they/it never forgot to appreciate the fans responsible for that success.

6) The university, once thought to have an exclusively wealthy student body, has been doing their/its best in recent years to admit students from more diverse backgrounds.

7) England, not always known for having great cuisine, has in recent years improved its/their image in the culinary world.

8) Although the company's profits declined, it/they remained determined not to fire any employees.

9) The board of directors have/has decided that they/it should take a more active role in watching over the day-to-day functions of the clinic.

10) The city, despite battling economic hardships, has/have tried its/their best to offer free events during the summer in order to attract more tourists to the area.

11) The College of William and Mary rank/ranks high in NCAA basketball.

12) The company, a leader in hiring women and minorities in executive positions, did its/their best to keep salaries equitable as well.

13) The team never made it to the playoff games; they were/it was a disappointment to once loyal fans.

14) The country has benefited from the tourism trade, but they still suffer/it still suffers from extreme poverty.

Capitalization

Directions: In each of the following sentences, circle the words that should be capitalized.

1) Did he ever vacation on lake winnipesaukee?

2) the french and indian war saw many major events, including a surrender at fort duquesne.

3) The law was championed by mayor bloomberg.

4) I always try to stay at the drake hotel when I visit chicago, but it's usually booked.

5) Mrs. Jacobson teaches my favorite class: history of literature.

6) the bibliography says that the information was taken from the library of alexandria.

7) Melissa loves the movie *diary of a wimpy kid*; she can recite every line.

8) Many people say that annie dillard's essay called "total eclipse" is one of the best essays ever written.

9) Last wednesday, I saw kristin chenoweth in the broadway production of *wicked*.

10) The school newspaper is called *the advocate*.

Pronouns

Directions: Make sure that the pronoun clearly matches its antecedent (the noun it replaces). Then, choose the best way to phrase the underlined portion of the sentence. If the original version is the best phrasing, select choice A.

1) I watched Yasmin and Julia from my position on the bridge high above the reservoir and felt my stomach drop as <u>she dove majestically into</u> the water from the rocky cliffs.
   a. she dove majestically into
   b. Julia dove majestically into
   c. the diving was done by she into
   d. the diving was done by her into

2) Laurie, Jimmy, and Aman were running home from school yesterday afternoon <u>when he tripped and fell.</u>
   a. when he tripped and fell.
   b. where it was Aman who tripped and fell.
   c. when it was him who tripped and fell.
   d. when Aman tripped and fell.

3) <u>In the prologue to the book, it explains</u> the importance of maintaining arts education.
   a. In the prologue to the book, it explains
   b. The prologue to the book explains
   c. It explains, the prologue to the book,
   d. It explains in the prologue to the book

4) Although Dresden was attacked and decimated by war, <u>the city has been rebuilt.</u>
   a. the city has been rebuilt.
   b. the city it has been rebuilt.
   c. some rebuilding has been done by them.
   d. the rebuilding of it has been done.

5) Local civilians were given cameras <u>to document any human rights abuses during it.</u>
   a. to document any human rights abuses during it.
   b. for the documenting of human rights abuses by them during it.
   c. to document it—human rights abuses.
   d. in order to document human rights abuses.

— Pronouns continued

6) Some people argue <u>as to it being unfair to offer tax breaks to those who can most afford to pay taxes.</u>

    a. as to it being unfair to offer tax breaks to those who can most afford to pay taxes.

    b. that it is unfair to offer tax breaks to those who can most afford to pay taxes.

    c. about the unfairness there is to offer tax breaks to those who can most afford to pay it.

    d. about government's unfairness when they offer tax breaks to those who can most afford to pay them.

Directions: Identify the pronouns in the following sentences, making sure to watch for agreement issues. Choose the pronoun that properly agrees with the noun it replaces.

7) A writer's first movie can be the most compelling because <u>they frequently draw/it frequently draws</u> upon the writer's own experiences.

8) Although people disparage the mobile phone, some rely upon <u>it/them</u> to facilitate their business dealings.

9) The printed magazine has struggled to maintain its business now that free online magazines have replaced <u>it/them</u> as a ready source of sports, news, fashion, and shopping information.

10) Most states impose penalties on drivers who are caught talking on <u>his or her/their</u> cell phones while driving.

11) For the hiker in the wilderness, each path along the way offers <u>its/their</u> own charm.

12) In the past, a teaching career was considered noble, but <u>they were/it was</u> not rewarded with high salaries.

13) Just as adults have very different personalities from one another, so do babies differ in <u>his or her/their</u> character traits.

14) The twin girls, Kendra and Keisha, began to cry at once, leading their mom to conclude that <u>she/they</u> needed a nap.

Pronoun Case

Directions: Circle the correct pronoun in the following sentences.

1) When my boss called Jerry and I/me into his office, we did not know whether to be honored or terrified.

2) Jared was shorter than I/me, but somehow he could jump much higher.

3) The age difference between my brothers and I/me made it difficult for me to hang out with them.

4) Before her roommate and her/she left on their road trip, Maria burned a CD of their favorite songs.

5) As my parents said goodbye to my twin and I/me, I saw tears form in my dad's eyes.

6) Deb may not be as outgoing as he/him, but I still think that she would do better at the job.

7) There was so much animosity between Will and she/her, it seemed unlikely that their group project would ever get done.

8) Tremendous flooding threatened to ruin the gardens that my sister and me/I worked so hard on all summer.

9) There has been friction between my lab partner and I/me because we have such different work styles.

10) Every time my boss says that another employee sold more items than I/me, it makes me want to give up rather than work harder.

11) England's teams won more matches than they/them but scored fewer goals overall in the tournament.

12) We both thought it was irresponsible of the doorman to give the key to Sarah and I/me without even checking our identification.

13) Regardless of whether you think that I sing as well as he/him, you didn't have to "boo" me off the stage.

14) If you give the recipe to either Virginia or I/me, we promise to bake that cake for you the next time we see you.

15) Niko and she/her walk down this street every day on their way to school, but they've never once said "hello" to Carrie and I/me.

Indefinite Pronouns

Directions: Circle the indefinite pronoun and then pick the proper pronoun and/ or verb form.

1) Every house is unique; each one offers (their/its) own type of structure and layout.

2) Each of them (is/are) going to do well on the test.

3) Both of the dogs (was/were) performing in the circus.

4) Everybody, even the bravest soldier in combat drills, (is/are) frightened by something.

5) Everyone, from the individual to the major company, (needs/need) to participate in recycling.

6) Few of my tomatoes (has/have) turned red yet.

7) Neither of their two daughters (is going/are going) to come to the vacation house this summer.

8) Every story included in the author's first two books (was/were) based on autobiographical details.

9) There comes a time in every dog's life when (it starts/they start) to think of (its/their) master as family.

10) Many of the trees (has, have) lost their leaves.

Active vs. Passive Voice

Directions: Select the active rather than the passive voice in the underlined portions of the following sentences.

1) The FCC distributes airwaves so that one transmission <u>will not interfere with another/is not interfered with by another.</u>

2) <u>Logic is made use of by mathematicians/Mathematicians use logic</u> to solve complex equations.

3) <u>Analogies are frequently relied upon by lawyers/Lawyers frequently rely upon analogies</u> to argue their cases before the court.

4) <u>Many of his supporters alleged/The allegation was made by many of his supporters</u> that he was innocent.

5) <u>Defenders of art education argue/The argument is made by those who defend art education</u> that art classes promote creative minds.

6) Because the employees were angry about management's refusal to give pay raises, <u>they threatened to strike/a threat of a strike was made by them.</u>

7) The new students appreciated the advice <u>the older students shared with them/shared with them by the older students.</u>

8) When scientists measure distances, <u>they often use/the use is often made by them of</u> the metric system.

9) When the art teacher arrived, <u>it was learned by her/she learned</u> that her students were away on the French class field trip.

10) <u>The player made the excuse/The excuse was made by the player</u> that he was suffering from the flu, but, in fact, he had stayed out late the night before the game.

11) Nobody liked it, but <u>the rule was made by the landlord/the landlord made the rule</u> that no pets could live in the apartment building.

12) <u>The prohibition on lighting candles in the dorms was made by the university/ The university prohibited lighting candles in the dorms</u> because of the risk of fire.

Tense

Directions: Choose the correct verb tense in the following sentences.

1) Mrs. Arvin (worked/works) in the school for 25 years before she retired last year.

2) He (hopes/hope) to build a tree house for his son's birthday.

3) Barbara (moved/moves) to Philadelphia four months ago.

4) Robin (builds/built) her daughter a scrapbook for her last birthday.

5) Lexie (hopes/hoped) to swim often this vacation with her friends.

6) They survived on food they (find/found) in the wild.

7) Not everyone (own/owned) cell phones in the past.

8) The rats multiplied and (make/made) problems for the settlers.

9) For a long time, stores (sell/sold) only one type of pepper.

10) She (order/ordered) five deli sandwiches.

11) For his daughter's birthday in two months, he (hopes/hoped) to have a dollhouse built.

12) Students (did/will) have a vacation in two weeks.

Directions: Fix the sentence so that all verb tenses match.

13) I ate dinner before he had entered the room.

14) If he tried harder, he could have won the game.

15) Yesterday, I had run in the race.

16) Before school today, I have two glasses of milk, and I ate four slices of bread.

17) Upon entering our house, I see that Hamlet, the boa constrictor, was gone.

18) Many people re-enter the job market when their youngest children started school.

— Tense continued

19) My father always tells me that honesty was the best policy.

20) Erma's brother always showed her that he has the utmost confidence in her.

Directions: Pick the correct tense.

21) Larry has (drank/drunk) his glass of milk.

22) She has always (did/done) her best.

23) The plate had (fallen/fell) to the ground.

24) Has John (went/gone) to work today?

25) Have you (ate/eaten) lunch today?

Linking, Helping, and Action Verbs

Directions: Indicate whether the verb is a linking (L), a helping (H), or an action (A) verb.

1) _____ The wind <u>is</u> very strong this afternoon.

2) _____ Moving slowly, the naturalist <u>was able</u> to absorb more details than could the average observer.

3) _____ The new information quickly <u>became</u> essential to Rachel's research.

4) _____ I <u>can</u> never decide which one to follow.

5) _____ Computers <u>adjust</u> the optics.

6) _____ The sky <u>appears</u> a lot darker than usual tonight.

7) _____ The mountain lion <u>is</u> a territorial animal.

8) _____ Sandy <u>turned</u> the corner at Fifth Street.

9) _____ The earlier you face the task, the sooner you <u>will</u> finish it.

10) _____ Bill <u>feels</u> uncomfortable giving speeches.

11) _____ The magician <u>made</u> the coin appear behind my ear.

12) _____ The tacos at the restaurant <u>tasted</u> good.

13) _____ A supernova <u>is</u> an exploding star.

14) _____ Avery <u>was</u> raised in Philadelphia.

15) _____ The grandfather <u>hugged</u> his grandchild before he got on the plane.

Verb Mood

Directions: Tell what mood the following sentences are in (imperative, interrogative, indicative, subjunctive, conditional).

1) _____ Cook me some pasta.

2) _____ I am thirsty.

3) _____ If Jen would have gone to the party, she would have run into her cousin.

4) _____ I wish I had something to do this afternoon.

5) _____ Should I go to the store?

6) _____ I will send you a text if I visit Seattle.

7) _____ Bring your books to the library.

8) _____ I wish it were winter.

9) _____ Yvonne was here.

10) _____ If she were here, she would agree with me.

11) _____ If he doesn't start working out, he will be cut from the baseball team.

12) _____ Would you prefer to go to the movies or bowling?

13) _____ If I would go, I would wear my new shoes.

14) _____ If I were in your position, I would go on the trip.

15) _____ Send me the report.

Verbals: Participle, Gerund, and Infinitive Phrases

Directions: Indicate in the sentences below whether the phrase is a participle, a gerund, or an infinitive phrase (P, G, or I). Write your answers in the spaces provided.

1) _____ <u>Drinking a cup of coffee</u> is the way he starts his day.

2) _____ The girls all want to go <u>to the concert.</u>

3) _____ Taylor tries <u>to practice the violin</u> on a regular basis.

4) _____ We left the room because we did not want to wake the <u>sleeping baby.</u>

5) _____ My father volunteered <u>to have the entire family</u> over for lunch.

6) _____ He was asked <u>to buy the ingredients</u> to make a pie.

7) _____ <u>Known as one of the best players in basketball,</u> Michael Jordan was inducted into the hall of fame.

8) _____ It is important <u>to eat three meals</u> every day.

9) _____ Greta was soon bored with <u>playing checkers.</u>

10) _____ <u>Taking a bath,</u> Cole washed his hair.

11) _____ <u>Opening the door,</u> Scott was surprised to see all of his friends yelling, "Surprise."

12) _____ <u>Playing soccer</u> every day is my idea of a great summer.

13) _____ <u>Knocking loudly on the door,</u> the teenager awakened his parents.

14) _____ Lindsey planned <u>to run for treasurer of her class.</u>

15) _____ Max enjoys <u>skiing the difficult trails.</u>

Fragments and Run-on Sentences

Directions: Identify each example below as a fragment (F), run-on sentence (ROS), or sentence (S). Write the letter on the line next to the example.

1) _____ Have you already visited that famous New York restaurant?

2) _____ At the end of the play.

3) _____ Let's open the presents, we want to see what you have been given.

4) _____ Last year, we wrote about some of the events.

5) _____ Again after all of the applause.

6) _____ Before they started their catering business.

7) _____ Please handle these expensive porcelain plates with care.

8) _____ The men fixing the shower need more time, they can charge us more if they need to do so.

9) _____ During the birthday party held at the park.

10) _____ Bring the empty bottles back from the factory they can be used again.

11) _____ While you get the mail, the rest of us can continue to set the table.

12) _____ There are too many people on this bus, who can take another one so this one is not so crowded?

13) _____ Several store managers tried to assist me finally I gave up.

14) _____ Early in the morning last September.

Adjectives

Directions: In the following sentences, circle the adjectives and underline the nouns they describe. Some of the sentences may have more than one set of adjectives and nouns.

1) Sarah did not understand why anyone would want to go outside and play in such hot weather.

2) These juicy strawberries are the best I've ever eaten.

3) My younger brother loves the new skateboard he got for his birthday.

4) The cold air stung his face as he walked through the blinding snow.

5) Many exciting movies revolve around thrilling adventures.

6) There are many interesting people in my math class.

7) My favorite aunt always brings me delicious cookies when she visits.

8) Dylan learned how to play two very difficult songs on his guitar.

9) Felipe's good grades showed how much hard work he put into his studies.

10) The small boat carefully navigated the humongous waves.

11) My teacher wore a green shirt to class on Friday.

12) During the difficult lesson, my friend politely asked her neighbor for help.

Adverbs

Directions: Circle the adverb in each of the sentences below.

1) Carla carefully fit the last piece into the puzzle.

2) Jen waited patiently for her friends to arrive.

3) Malcolm stopped suddenly to listen.

4) I will visit my grandparents tomorrow.

5) Leslie left the room and angrily slammed the door.

6) Evan quickly read the book.

7) Ted left the party early.

8) Lily and Raj played here.

9) My uncle snores loudly.

10) Kevin, will you come over here?

11) We spent the day sitting lazily by the beach.

12) Max accidentally slipped on the wet floor.

Prepositions

Directions: Circle the prepositional phrases and underline the prepositions in the following sentences.

1) The parrots on his shoulder were more talkative than the man.

2) Not a single option on the two chalkboard menus was appealing to the child.

3) The introduction of the product to consumers was delayed by new FDA regulations.

4) She was tired, but she read to her sister until the thunderstorm subsided.

5) Contemporary musicals draw upon popular styles of music.

6) Many citizens are passionate about recycling; yet, it can be difficult to sort garbage into the glass, paper, and trash bins.

7) Beneath the Earth's surface live billions of microscopic organisms.

8) Located past an imposing iron gate, the mansion received very few visitors on Halloween.

9) Findings in the report by scientists at the university suggest that water pollution throughout the state is gradually being fixed.

10) The house across the street from the Richardsons' has been empty all summer.

11) Happiness for me is a warm summer day.

12) He either closed his eyes or ducked down in his seat during the scary parts of the movie.

13) The hotel staff collected various items left within the party room after the wedding, including the flower arrangements and a pair of silver high-heeled shoes.

14) The contrast between the wealth of the company executives and the poverty of the workers led to an unhappy work environment.

Dangling and Misplaced Modifiers

Directions: Choose the best way to phrase the underlined portion of each sentence below. If the original phrasing is the best version, choose choice A.

1) Free at last from imperial rule, <u>the idea of a strong central government made representatives at the Constitutional Convention wary.</u>

    a. the idea of a strong central government made representatives at the Constitutional Convention wary.

    b. a great number of the representative's wariness over a strong central government made them cautious.

    c. a great number of representatives attending the Constitutional Convention were wary of a strong central government.

    d. the wariness of the representatives about a strong central government made many of them cautious.

2) Known for its stunning vistas, <u>the Grand Canyon attracts many visitors each day.</u>

    a. the Grand Canyon attracts many visitors each day.

    b. the Grand Canyon's views attract many visitors each day.

    c. many visitors are attracted to the Grand Canyon to enjoy it daily.

    d. the Grand Canyon's vistas attract many visitors each day.

3) Looking down through the glass floor of the tower, <u>the girl could see the beautiful city that was to be her new hometown.</u>

    a. the girl could see the beautiful city that was to be her new hometown.

    b. the city that was to be the girl's new home town looked beautiful.

    c. the girl's views of the beautiful city that would be her new home became clear.

    d. the girl, seeing the beautiful city that was to be her new home.

4) <u>Born in New York, the author's first novel</u> drew upon the city's many diverse neighborhoods.

    a. Born in New York, the author's first novel

    b. Born in New York, the first novel by the author

    c. The first novel which was by the author who was born in New York City and

    d. The first novel by the New York-born author

— Dangling and Misplaced Modifiers continued

5) Careful to create interesting characters as well as a strong plot, <u>the award-winning mystery writer authored books that were</u> both entertaining and intellectually challenging.

    a. the award-winning mystery writer authored books that were

    b. the award-winning mystery writer's books were

    c. the books of the award-winning mystery writer were

    d. the award-winning mystery writer who authored books

6) Wandering through new cities, <u>the tourists relied heavily on their maps and guidebooks.</u>

    a. the tourists relied heavily on their maps and guidebooks.

    b. the tourists' maps and guidebooks were essential to the tourists.

    c. the maps and guidebooks were what the tourists relied on.

    d. the tourists who relied heavily on their maps and guidebooks.

7) <u>Buying one in every color, the style of the dress flattered the girl.</u>

    a. Buying one in every color, the style of the dress flattered the girl.

    b. The style of the dress, because it was flattering, was bought by the girl in every color.

    c. Because the dress flattered the girl, she decided to buy one in every color.

    d. Buying one in every color, was because of the girl's opinion that the style flattered her.

8) Preoccupied with excessive displays of wealth, <u>the failure of the company could be blamed on its own greed.</u>

    a. the failure of the company could be blamed on its own greed.

    b. the executives of the company brought about its failure.

    c. the executive's own greed brought about the company's failure.

    d. the company failed which was because of its own executives.

— Dangling and Misplaced Modifiers continued

9) Walking across the tightrope for the first time without a net, <u>the young circus performer felt a mixture of terror and exhilaration.</u>

    a. the young circus performer felt a mixture of terror and exhilaration.

    b. a mixture of terror and exhilaration filled the young circus performer's mind.

    c. the young circus performer's mind was filled with a mixture of terror and exhilaration.

    d. the young circus performer felt both terror in addition to also feeling exhilaration.

10) Although trained on Broadway, <u>his current role in a movie will lead to more fame for the actor.</u>

    a. his current role in a movie will lead to more fame for the actor.

    b. the actor's current role in a movie will lead to more fame for him.

    c. the actor will gain more fame for his current movie role.

    d. the fame of the actor will be more for his current role in a movie.

11) Located in the heart of Paris, <u>many tourists to the city visit Notre Dame.</u>

    a. many tourists to the city visit Notre Dame.

    b. is Notre Dame where many tourists visit it.

    c. Notre Dame's popularity is appealing to many tourists.

    d. Notre Dame is popular with many tourists.

12) Distracted by the extra luggage, <u>Michael failed to notice the pickpockets.</u>

    a. Michael failed to notice the pickpockets.

    b. the pickpockets went unnoticed by Michael.

    c. was the attention of Michael, therefore he failed to notice the pickpockets.

    d. the pickpockets were able to go unnoticed by Michael.

— Dangling and Misplaced Modifiers continued

Directions: Rewrite the sentence, fixing the modification errors.

13) Keep to the right of the monument of Lincoln driving out of town.

14) That's my picture on the floor that you're stepping on.

15) The women and children were herded into the house sale with amazing rudeness.

16) I like the doughnuts on the table with the chocolate frosting.

17) I have almost studied for this test for two hours.

18) We could see smoke rising from our neighbor's chimney with a pair of binoculars.

19) They could see the blimp sitting on the front lawn.

20) We had a hamburger after the movie, which was too well-done.

21) Our phone almost rang fifteen times last night.

22) I read that Chuck Yeager was a pilot who broke the sound barrier in the library.

23) Sally selected a doughnut from the bakery filled with chocolate cream.

24) The fire squad staged a fire drill during class without warning.

Conjunctions

Directions: Circle the conjunction in each of the following sentences. Choose the best way to phrase the underlined portion of the sentence. If the original version is the best phrasing, choose A.

1) Not only was she the first member of her family to go to college, <u>and she also received a scholarship.</u>

    a. and she also received a scholarship.

    b. nor even less impressive was that she received a scholarship.

    c. but receiving a scholarship too.

    d. but she also received a scholarship.

2) Although the disputes about ownership of the song temporarily quieted, <u>but the disputes have now reappeared.</u>

    a. but the disputes have now reappeared.

    b. the disputes have now reappeared.

    c. and the disputes have now reappeared.

    d. however the disputes have now reappeared.

3) Neither Chen <u>nor his brother appears to be particularly shy.</u>

    a. nor his brother appears to be particularly shy.

    b. nor his brother appear to be particularly shy.

    c. or his brothers appear like they are particularly shy.

    d. and even less his brother appears to be particularly shy.

4) We learn a lot about history from books, <u>but oral histories having the ability to provide even more nuanced information.</u>

    a. but oral histories having the ability to provide even more nuanced information.

    b. and oral histories having the ability to provide even more nuanced information.

    c. but, even more so, oral histories having the ability to provide nuanced information.

    d. but oral histories have the ability to provide even more nuanced information.

5) Facing formidable odds, the general tried to avoid being trapped, <u>but failing.</u>

    a. but failing.

    b. but he failed.

    c. and yet failing.

    d. but it failed.

— Conjunctions continued

6) <u>Neither the chairman or the vice chairman of the committee thinks</u> that the corporation has enough information on which to make a decision.

    a. Neither the chairman or the vice chairman of the committee thinks
    b. Neither the chairman or the vice chairman of the committee think
    c. Neither the chairman nor the vice chairman of the committee thinks
    d. Neither the chairman nor the vice chairman of the committee think

7) Either the threat of punishment <u>or her moral conscience stopped the girl</u> from following the others when they broke their curfew.

    a. or her moral conscience stopped the girl
    b. and additionally her moral conscience stopped
    c. or having a moral conscience which stopped the girl
    d. or the risk of her moral conscience stopping

8) Whereas most dogs cause my brother to sneeze, <u>but our dog proving to be hypoallergenic.</u>

    a. but our dog proving to be hypoallergenic.
    b. but our dog is hypoallergenic.
    c. our dog is hypoallergenic.
    d. the hypoallergenic characteristic of our dog is the opposite.

9) Until the bus came to a halt, <u>neither the driver nor the passenger were aware</u> that a cat had come aboard.

    a. neither the driver nor the passenger were aware
    b. neither the driver nor the passenger was aware
    c. neither the driver or the passenger was aware
    d. neither the driver or even less so the passenger was aware

10) At the end of a long day, it is sometimes tempting to <u>collapse on the sofa, turn on the television, and generally stop thinking.</u>

    a. collapse on the sofa, turn on the television, and generally stop thinking.
    b. collapse on the sofa, turning on the television, and generally to stop thinking.
    c. collapse on the sofa, turn on the television, and all thinking is stopped.
    d. either collapse on the sofa, turn on the television, and generally stop thinking.

Comparisons

Directions: Choose the best way to phrase the underlined portion of each sentence below. If the original phrasing produces the best sentence, select choice A.

1) The composer's issue was the same <u>as many young songwriter:</u> She needed to decide whether to try to create music he loved or music that would sell records.

    a. as many young songwriters

    b. as that of many young songwriters

    c. as being that of other young songwriters

    d. of which faced other young songwriters

2) Because she worked hard and had done well in her previous history classes, Maria made the assumption that her <u>grade would be higher than the other students</u> in the class.

    a. her grade would be higher than the other students

    b. of the other students her grade was the higher

    c. of all the students she was the highest grade

    d. her grade would be higher than those of the other students

3) The methods used by the brain to solve problems <u>are almost the same as a computer.</u>

    a. are almost the same as a computer.

    b. are nearly the same almost as those used by a computer.

    c. which are similar to those used by a computer.

    d. are almost the same as those used by a computer.

4) With a little bit of effort, a home-cooked meal, using fresh ingredients, can sometimes <u>taste better than an expensive restaurant.</u>

    a. taste better than an expensive restaurant.

    b. taste even more better than an expensive restaurant.

    c. taste better than a meal from an expensive restaurant.

    d. taste better than a more expensive restaurant.

5) The home run total for the winner of this year's competition <u>was greater than the sum of the previous two years.</u>

    a. was greater than the sum of the previous two years.

    b. was the most greatest sum of the previous two years.

    c. was greater than the sum of the winning totals from the previous two years.

    d. was the greater sum than that which was totaled in the previous two years.

— Comparisons continued

6) The author's stories drew more upon her experiences studying abroad <u>than upon those of her rural upbringing.</u>

    a. than upon those of her rural upbringing.
    b. than her rural upbringing would do.
    c. than most of her rural upbringing had done.
    d. than her rural upbringing did.

7) Only slightly longer than the other jumps <u>was the athlete from Ghana whose jumps won the competition.</u>

    a. was the athlete from Ghana whose jumps won the competition.
    b. were the athlete from Ghana whose jumps won the competition.
    c. being those of the athlete from Ghana who won the competition.
    d. were those of the athlete from Ghana who won the competition.

8) In some circles, furniture made by rural Asian craftsmen <u>has become as popular as European furniture makers.</u>

    a. has become as popular as European furniture makers.
    b. has become as popular as European furniture.
    c. who, becoming as popular as European furniture.
    d. , as much as European furniture, are becoming popular.

9) The depth of meaning in his novels compares favorably <u>to other authors.</u>

    a. to other authors.
    b. to that in the works of other authors.
    c. than that in other authors.
    d. than with other authors' works.

10) The racecar driver could drive faster and more accurately <u>than could the average driver.</u>

    a. than could the average driver.
    b. than the average car.
    c. unlike the average driver's car.
    d. in comparison to the average driver's car.

Sentence Structure

Directions: Identify each sentence below as either a simple, compound, or complex sentence, and write your answer on the line before the sentence.

1) _____ The kids stood in the lunch line, and the cafeteria worker put food on everyone's tray.

2) _____ It snowed the entire week.

3) _____ Even though Jason looked everywhere, he was unable to find his missing pencil case.

4) _____ The math teacher tried out a new set of questions, and all of the students really enjoyed them.

5) _____ Caitlyn hopes to visit her aunt this summer.

6) _____ The school bus pulled up to the curb, and five students got off.

7) _____ The kids were quiet while a guest speaker taught a lesson.

8) _____ Is there school today?

9) _____ After class ended, the kids ran outside for recess.

10) _____ The teacher handed back the test, and all the students watched her nervously.

11) _____ If it were not for the pleadings of my friend, I would not be here.

12) _____ All textbooks older than five years can be stored here.

13) _____ You can stay after school, or you can go home.

14) _____ She finished the test before time was up.

15) _____ At the same time each night, the bells play out their mournful tune.

Subject/Verb Agreement

Directions: After determining whether the subject is singular or plural, match the subject to the correct verb form.

1) Their irritation over the annoying sounds has/have ruined the girls' ability to concentrate on the test.

2) The school, famous for its successful graduates, were/was able to charge a high tuition.

3) Noisier than most dogs, my poodle, French Fries, has/have bad etiquette at the dog run.

4) His techniques for trying to solve the equation on the math homework was/were mostly unsuccessful.

5) The neighbors from the big house diagonally across the street from my sister is/are famous for the party they throw every summer.

6) The number of awards that will be given this year for movies remain/remains the same, although the number of nominees has increased.

7) To the astute observer, the beauty in good paintings is/are often tied to the message delivered.

8) The best time of the year for harvesting the vegetables is/are in the late summer.

9) The entire population, even the richest of citizens, was/were worried about the financial crisis.

10) Early each morning, when the clock strikes 6:30, students around the country wake/wakes up and prepare to get ready for school.

Apostrophes

Directions: Pay attention to the apostrophes in the following sentences.
Decide whether you need the apostrophe and if it is properly placed.
Then choose the best way to phrase the underlined portion of each sentence.
If the original phrasing is the best version, choose A.

1) By the end of the tennis match, <u>both player's arms</u> required deep tissue massages.

    a. both player's arms
    b. both players' arms
    c. both players arm's
    d. both players arms'

2) The city is popular for <u>its culture and it's nightlife.</u>

    a. its culture and it's nightlife.
    b. it's culture and its nightlife.
    c. it's culture and it's nightlife.
    d. its culture and its nightlife.

3) Fire is one of <u>humankind's earliest inventions.</u>

    a. humankind's earliest inventions.
    b. humankinds' earliest inventions.
    c. humankinds earliest invention's.
    d. humankinds earliest inventions'.

4) Membership on the debate team caused students to challenge <u>one anothers basic assumption's and prejudice's.</u>

    a. one anothers basic assumption's and prejudice's.
    b. one anothers' basic assumptions and prejudices.
    c. one another's basic assumptions and prejudices.
    d. one another's basic assumptions' and prejudices'.

5) When we see the troupe perform, we appreciate <u>their hard work</u> and training.

    a. their hard work
    b. it's hard work
    c. its hard work
    d. its' hard work

— Apostrophes continued

6) I belong to a small club; in fact, <u>it's in danger of losing it's entire membership</u> to a nearby larger club.

    a. it's in danger of losing it's entire membership
    b. it's in danger of losing its entire membership
    c. its in danger of losing it's entire membership
    d. its in danger of losing its entire membership

7) <u>Egyptian musicians wrote all the music for the movie's soundtrack.</u>

    a. Egyptian musicians wrote all the music for the movie's soundtrack.
    b. Egyptians' musicians wrote all the music for the movie's soundtrack.
    c. Egyptian musician's wrote all the music for the movie's soundtrack.
    d. Egyptian musicians wrote all the music for the movies soundtrack.

8) I rode on <u>my horses back and admired it's strength</u> and beauty.

    a. my horses back and admired it's strength
    b. my horse's back and admired it's strength
    c. my horses back and admired its strength
    d. my horse's back and admired its strength

9) <u>The womens' soccer team was more successful than the men's team</u> this year.

    a. The womens' soccer team was more successful than the men's team
    b. The womens' soccer team was more successful than the mens' team
    c. The women's soccer team was more successful than the men's team
    d. The women's soccer team was more successful than the mens' team

10) <u>Who's mittens are lying on that table?</u>

    a. Who's mittens are lying on that table?
    b. Whose mittens are lying that on the table?
    c. Who's mitten's are lying on that on the table?
    d. Whose mittens' are lying on that table?

Commas and Semicolons

Directions: Read the following sentences. Choose the best version of the under-lined portion of the sentence. If the original version is the best one, choose choice A.

1) In the <u>early morning. Just before</u> the sun rose, I set off for the airport.

    a. early morning. Just before

    b. early morning; just before

    c. early morning, it was just before

    d. early morning, just before

2) Kim's coursework illuminated the difficulties <u>of solving world problems, but she</u> retained her idealism.

    a. of solving world problems, but she

    b. of, solving world problems but she

    c. of, solving world problems, but she

    d. of solving, world problems, but she

3) I get tired in the <u>late afternoon, however, drinking coffee</u> only makes me jumpy.

    a. late afternoon, however, drinking coffee

    b. late afternoon however drinking coffee

    c. late afternoon; however, drinking, coffee

    d. late afternoon; however, drinking coffee

4) The coach had a <u>good reputation, she was known</u> for getting the most out of her players.

    a. good reputation, she was known

    b. good reputation; she was known

    c. good reputation, she, was known

    d. good reputation. She, was known

5) <u>Trying as hard as she could, the rope still seemed</u> impossible to climb.

    a. Trying as hard as she could, the rope still seemed

    b. Trying as hard as she could, the girl, still found the rope

    c. Trying as hard as she could, the girl still found the rope

    d. Trying, as hard as she could, the rope still seemed

— Commas and Semicolons continued

6) <u>For an entire year, the man ate only soup, salad, and dessert.</u>

    a. For an entire year, the man ate only soup, salad, and dessert.

    b. For an entire year, the man ate only soup salad, and dessert.

    c. For an entire year, the man ate only soup salad and dessert.

    d. For an entire year the man ate, only soup, salad, and dessert.

7) <u>He didn't want to be late, therefore, he would not be.</u>

    a. He didn't want to be late, therefore, he would not be.

    b. He didn't want to be late therefore, he would not be.

    c. He didn't want to be late therefore he would not be.

    d. He didn't want to be late; therefore, he would not be.

8) <u>The drama club had a tough year ahead. Lacking the funding</u> it needed for its productions.

    a. The drama club had a tough year ahead. Lacking the funding

    b. The drama club had a tough year ahead, lacking the funding

    c. The drama club, had a tough year ahead, lacking the funding

    d. The drama club, had a tough year ahead lacking the funding

9) <u>The pasta with vegetables the only vegetarian item on the menu, happened to be</u> my favorite dish.

    a. The pasta with vegetables the only vegetarian item on the menu, happened to be

    b. The pasta with vegetables the only vegetarian item on, the menu, happened to be

    c. The pasta, with vegetables the only vegetarian item on the menu happened to be

    d. The pasta with vegetables, the only vegetarian item on the menu, happened to be

10) <u>She wore purple, and red to school each day.</u>

    a. She wore purple, and red to school each day.

    b. She wore purple and red, to school each day.

    c. She wore purple and red to school each day.

    d. She, wore purple and red to school each day.

Punctuation: Dashes, Colons, Semicolons, Commas, Parentheses, and Ellipses

Directions: Choose the best way to phrase the underlined portion of each sentence. If the original phrasing is the best version, choose choice A.

1) The organization that owned the auditorium canceled the contract; just a week before the performance.

   a. canceled the contract; just
   b. canceled the contract. Just
   c. canceled the contract, however
   d. canceled the contract just

2) She did not always welcome visitors. Since years ago she was robbed by an electrician.

   a. visitors. Since years ago,
   b. visitors; since years ago
   c. visitors; years ago,
   d. visitors, although, years ago

3) She asked me if the snake was dangerous; I reassured her that it was not.

   a. dangerous; I reassured her
   b. dangerous, I reassured her
   c. dangerous; reassuring her
   d. dangerous, where I reassured her

4) The teacher is famous around the world for the relaxation methods she developed, they make use of music and coordinated deep-breathing exercises.

   a. she developed, they make use of
   b. she developed; making use of
   c. which, making use of
   d. she developed; they make use of

— Punctuation: Dashes, Colons, Semicolons, Commas, Parentheses, and Ellipses continued

5) When she became editor of her <u>school newspaper; the girl resolved to address issues of bullying</u> that she saw on her campus.

    a. school newspaper; the girl resolved to address issues of bullying

    b. school newspaper, it was when the girl resolved to address issues of bullying

    c. school newspaper, the girl resolved to address issues of bullying

    d. school newspaper; a resolve made by the girl was to address issues of bullying

6) The actor was not born in <u>New York, he left his native state to pursue his dreams</u> of a Broadway career.

    a. New York, he left his native state to pursue his dreams

    b. New York; he left his native state to pursue his dreams

    c. New York, it was why he left his native state to pursue his dreams

    d. New York; leaving his native state to pursue his dreams

7) My Mom was deciding between three different <u>types of cars: SUV, van, and sedan.</u>

    a. types of cars; SUV, van, and sedan.

    b. types of cars SUV, van, and sedan.

    c. types of cars: SUV, van, and sedan.

    d. types, of cars: SUV, van, and sedan.

8) <u>In general a show-off is someone, who likes to brag about herself.</u>

    a. In general a show-off is someone, who likes to brag about herself.

    b. In general: a show-off is someone who likes to brag about herself.

    c. In general, a show-off is someone who likes to brag about herself.

    d. In general, a show-off is someone who likes to brag, about herself.

9) Going to the <u>gym is a great workout, I try to go every day.</u>

    a. Going to the gym is a great workout, I try to go every day.

    b. Going to the gym is a great workout; I try to go every day.

    c. Going to the gym—is a great workout—I try to go every day.

    d. Going to the gym, is a great workout; I try to go every day.

— Punctuation: Dashes, Colons, Semicolons, Commas, Parentheses, and Ellipses continued

10) <u>There was only one thing left to do study</u> as much as possible before the test.

   a. There was only one thing left to do study as much as possible before the test.

   b. There was, only one thing left to do, study as much as possible before the test.

   c. There was only: one thing left to do study as much as possible before the test.

   d. There was only one thing left to do: study as much as possible before the test.

Directions: In the sentences below, add one of the following punctuation marks: an ellipsis, parentheses, a colon, a semicolon, or a dash.

11) Last summer, Emma wrote and wrote and then wrote some more until her novel was finally complete.

12) My baseball mitt autographed by New York Yankee Derek Jeter is displayed in a glass case.

13) Five of my six aunts were musicians, and the other in case you care to know became a cardiologist.

14) The television reporter traveled to cities in different parts of the United States San Diego, Minneapolis, Austin, and New York.

15) One of the most common ingredients in Thai cooking is curry paste it comes in several varieties.

Wordiness

Directions: Revise the following sentences for economy of expression.

1) She constantly irritates and bothers me all the time.

2) He spoke to me concerning the matter of my future.

3) Is it a true fact that the ozone layer is being depleted?

4) Let's go at 2:00 a.m. in the morning.

5) Consequently, as a result of the election, the state will have its first female governor.

6) My father's habitual custom is to watch the sun set in the west.

7) Vishal picked up a brush at the age of ten years old and hasn't stopped painting since.

8) Research shows that avid sports fans not only suffer from depression less, but they are also generally healthier, too, than those not interested in sports.

9) His field of work is that of a chemist.

10) For the second time, the cough recurred again.

Diction

Directions: Choose the correct answer.

1) She _____ her birthday present. (accepted/excepted)

2) My mom's advice did not _____ me. (affect/effect)

3) The _____ of the new technology is amazing. (affect/effect)

4) My brother Kevin is younger _____ I. (than/then)

5) We lived in Chicago; _____ we moved to Los Angeles. (than/then)

6) She served _____ many dishes for lunch. (to/too/two)

7) That is _____ house on Foothill Lane. (their/there/they're)

8) The project directions tell you to _____ at least two articles in your research. (site/cite)

9) The teacher said we _____ use a calculator to do the math problems. (may/can)

10) I _____ do 30 sit-ups in a row. (may/can)

11) I will _____ your wallet on your desk after I borrow five dollars. (lie/lay)

12) You can _____ down and go to bed; I know you're tired after having two soccer games today. (lie/lay)

13) My five-month-old nephew just learned how to _____ up without any help from his mother. (sit/set)

14) We always _____ our recycling bin just past our driveway so that it will get picked up on Tuesdays. (sit/set)

15) I should eat _____ bagels. (fewer/less)

16) I should drink _____ orange juice. (fewer/less)

17) _____ me the books so that I can do my homework. (Bring/Take)

18) _____ these books to the library. (Bring/Take)

19) Growing _____ all the sunflowers were weeds. (among/between)

20) Many crabs feed _____ the ocean and the sand dunes. (among/between)

Parallelism

Directions: Watch for the hand holders (correlative conjunctions) in the following sentences. Choose the best way to phrase the underlined portion of each sentence below. If the original phrasing is the best version, select choice A.

1) To succeed in college, you must be willing not only to work hard—perhaps harder than ever before—and also to manage your time well.

    a. and also to manage your time well.
    b. and in addition to manage your time well.
    c. however to manage your time well.
    d. but also to manage your time well.

2) According to some research, many high schools will graduate students who can neither read the newspaper or write a cover letter for a job application.

    a. or write a cover letter for a job application.
    b. nor write a cover letter for a job application.
    c. or even write a cover letter for a job application.
    d. and forget about writing a cover letter for a job application.

3) Many claim that it is possible both to grow a successful company while maintaining profits.

    a. while maintaining profits.
    b. in addition to maintaining its profitability.
    c. plus to maintain its profitability.
    d. and to maintain its profitability.

4) The school required that students either keep their backpacks in their school lockers and alternatively in their gym lockers.

    a. in their school lockers and alternatively in their gym lockers.
    b. in their school lockers and the other choice was in their gym lockers.
    c. in their school lockers or in their gym lockers.
    d. in their school lockers in addition to the choice of their gym lockers.

5) The director of the a cappella group not only had to direct rehearsals, but also had to arrange the music for the group.

    a. but also had to arrange the music for the group.
    b. and also had the responsibility to arrange music for the group.
    c. additionally she had to be responsible for arranging the group's music.
    d. as well as she had to arrange music for the group.

— Parallelism continued

6) The critics agreed that neither the words <u>or even the lyrics to the song</u> seemed to fit the theme of the movie.
   a. or even the lyrics to the song
   b. and the lyrics to the song
   c. nor the lyrics to the song
   d. and even less the lyrics to the song

7) Friends of <u>both the bride or the groom received welcome baskets</u> with tickets to a Broadway show.
   a. both the bride or the groom received welcome baskets
   b. either the bride and the groom received welcome baskets
   c. both the bride as well as the groom received welcome baskets
   d. both the bride and the groom received welcome baskets

Directions: In the following sentences, correct any problems with parallel structure.

8) Filing taxes is about as much fun as when you watch paint dry.

9) Cinderella swept the floors, washed the windows and she mopped the kitchen herself.

10) Parents often prefer to pay high school taxes then to the paying of high tuition.

11) Fran spends her free time reading, listening to music, and she works in the garden.

12) Students at the college often earn spending money by babysitting and some of them mow lawns.

Idioms

Directions: Identify the idioms. Write a revised version in the space provided. One sentence is correct as is.

1) I just threw the ball on Diego.

2) I really hope my English teacher will comply to my request for an extra day to write my paper.

3) His ability to understand the problem is different than mine.

4) Because of his preoccupation in traveling all over the world, Justin bought a copy of National Geographic.

5) I am very happy at my friend's behavior.

6) When Lucy returned home, she felt as though she'd never been away.

7) The invaders were horrible people, men who had absolutely no concern for human life.

8) It was definitely impossible for the man to separate reality with fantasy.

Answer Keys

Parts of Speech Review, pages 80–81

1) n
2) v
3) n
4) advb
5) int
6) pro
7) advb
8) adj
9) c
10) pro
11) n
12) v
13) n
14) int
15) prep
16) n
17) v
18) int
19) adj
20) n
21) v
22) c
23) pro
24) prep
25) int

Collective Nouns, page 82

1) species, its
2) country, its
3) deer, its
4) country, it was
5) band, it

6) university, its
7) England, its
8) company, it
9) board of directors, has, it
10) city, has, its
11) The College of William and Mary, ranks
12) The company, its
13) team, it was
14) country, it still suffers

Capitalization, page 83

1) Lake Winnipesaukee
2) The French, Indian War, Fort Duquesne
3) Mayor Bloomberg
4) Drake Hotel, Chicago
5) History, Literature
6) The, Library of Alexandria
7) Diary, Wimpy, Kid
8) Annie Dillard's, "Total Eclipse"
9) Wednesday, Kristin Chenoweth, Broadway, Wicked
10) The Advocate

Pronouns, pages 84–85

1) b. Julia dove majestically into
2) d. when Aman tripped and fell
3) b. The prologue to the book explains
4) a. the city has been rebuilt.
5) d. in order to document human rights abuses.
6) b. that it is unfair to offer tax breaks to those who can most afford to pay taxes.
7) it frequently draws
8) it
9) it
10) their
11) its
12) it was
13) their
14) they

Pronoun Case, page 86

1) me
2) I
3) me
4) she
5) me
6) he
7) her
8) I
9) me
10) I
11) they
12) me
13) he
14) me
15) she, me

Indefinite Pronouns, page 87

1) each, its
2) Each, is
3) Both, were
4) Everybody, is
5) Everyone, needs
6) Few, have
7) Neither, is going
8) Every, was
9) every, it starts, its
10) Many, have

Active vs. Passive Voice, page 88

1) will not interfere with another
2) Mathematicians use logic
3) Lawyers frequently rely upon analogies
4) Many of his supporters alleged
5) Defenders of art education argue
6) they threatened to strike
7) the older students shared with them
8) they often use
9) she learned

10) The player made the excuse

11) the landlord made the rule

12) The university prohibited lighting candles in the dorms

Tense, pages 89–90

1) worked
2) hopes
3) moved
4) built
5) hopes
6) found
7) owned
8) made
9) sold
10) ordered
11) hopes
12) will
13) ate ➞ had eaten
14) tried ➞ had tried
15) had run ➞ ran
16) have ➞ had
17) was ➞ is
18) started➞ start
19) was ➞ is
20) showed ➞ shows
21) drunk
22) done
23) fallen
24) gone
25) eaten

Linking, Helping, and Action Verbs, page 91

1) L
2) H
3) L
4) H
5) A
6) L
7) L
8) A

9) H
10) L
11) A
12) L
13) L
14) H
15) A

Verb Mood, page 92

1) imperative
2) indicative
3) conditional
4) subjunctive
5) interrogative
6) conditional
7) imperative
8) subjunctive
9) indicative
10) conditional
11) conditional
12) interrogative
13) conditional
14) subjunctive
15) imperative

Verbals: Participle, Gerund, and Infinitive Phrases, page 93

1) G
2) I
3) I
4) P
5) I
6) I
7) P
8) I
9) G
10) P
11) P
12) G
13) P

14) I
15) G

Fragments and Run-on Sentences, page 94

1) S
2) F
3) ROS
4) S
5) F
6) F
7) S
8) ROS
9) F
10) ROS
11) S
12) ROS
13) ROS
14) F

Adjectives, page 95

1) hot weather
2) juicy strawberries, best
3) younger brother, new skateboard
4) cold air, blinding snow
5) exciting movies, thrilling adventures
6) interesting people, math class
7) favorite aunt, delicious cookies
8) two, difficult, songs
9) good grades, hard work
10) small boat, humongous waves
11) green shirt
12) difficult lesson

Adverbs, page 96

1) carefully
2) patiently
3) suddenly
4) tomorrow
5) angrily
6) quickly

7) early

8) here

9) loudly

10) here

11) lazily

12) accidentally

Prepositions, page 97

1) <u>on</u> his shoulder

2) <u>on</u> the two chalkboard menus, <u>to</u> the child

3) <u>of</u> the product, <u>to</u> consumers, <u>by</u> new FDA regulations

4) <u>to</u> her sister, <u>until</u> the thunderstorm subsided

5) <u>upon</u> popular styles, <u>of</u> music

6) <u>about</u> recycling, <u>into</u> the glass, paper, and trash bins

7) <u>beneath</u> the Earth's surface, <u>of</u> microscopic organisms

8) <u>past</u> an imposing iron gate, <u>on</u> Halloween

9) <u>in</u> the report, <u>by</u> scientists, <u>at</u> the university, <u>throughout</u> the state

10) <u>across</u> the street, <u>from</u> the Richardsons'

11) <u>for</u> me

12) <u>in</u> his seat, <u>during</u> the scary parts, <u>of</u> the movie

13) <u>within</u> the party room, <u>after</u> the wedding, <u>of</u> silver high-heeled shoes

14) <u>between</u> the wealth, <u>of</u> the company executives, <u>of</u> the workers, <u>to</u> an unhappy work environment

Dangling and Misplaced Modifiers, pages 98–101

1) c. a great number of representatives attending the Constitutional Convention were wary of a strong central government.

2) a. the Grand Canyon attracts many visitors each day.

3) a. the girl could see the beautiful city that was to be her new hometown.

4) d. The first novel by the New York-born author

5) a. the award-winning mystery writer authored books that were

6) a. the tourists relied heavily on their maps and guidebooks.

7) c. Because the dress flattered the girl, she decided to buy one in every color.

8) b. the executives of the company brought about its failure.

9) a. the young circus performer felt a mixture of terror and exhilaration.

10) c. the actor will gain more fame for his current movie role.

11) d. Notre Dame is popular with many tourists.

12) a. Michael failed to notice the pickpockets.

13) Driving out of town, keep to the right of Lincoln's monument.

14) That's my picture on the floor, which you're stepping on. OR You're stepping on my picture on the floor.
15) The women and children were herded with amazing rudeness into the house sale.
16) I like the chocolate frosted doughnuts on the table.
17) I have studied for this test for almost two hours.
18) We could see with a pair of binoculars smoke rising from our neighbor's chimney.
19) While sitting on the front lawn, they could see the blimp.
20) After the movie, we had a hamburger, which was too well-done.
21) Last night, our phone rang almost fifteen times.
22) In the library, I read that Chuck Yeager was a pilot who broke the sound barrier.
23) From the bakery, Sally selected a doughnut filled with chocolate cream.
24) During class, the fire squad staged a fire drill without warning.

Conjunctions, pages 102–103

1) d. but she also received a scholarship, but
2) b. the disputes have now reappeared, although
3) a. nor his brother appears to be particularly shy, nor
4) d. but oral histories have the ability to provide even more nuanced information, but
5) b. but he failed, but
6) c. Neither the chairman nor the vice-chairman of the committee thinks, nor
7) a. or her moral conscience stopped the girl, or
8) c. our dog is hypoallergenic, whereas
9) b. neither the driver nor the passenger was aware, neither
10) a. collapse on the sofa, turn on the television, and generally stop thinking, and

Comparisons, pages 104–105

1) b. as that of many young songwriters
2) d. her grade would be higher than those of the other students
3) d. are almost the same as those used by a computer.
4) c. taste better than a meal from an expensive restaurant.
5) c. was greater than the sum of the winning totals from the previous two years.
6) a. than upon those of her rural upbringing.
7) d. were those of the athlete from Ghana who won the competition.
8) b. has become as popular as European furniture.
9) b. to that in the works of other authors.
10) a. than could the average driver.

Sentence Structure, page 106

1) compound
2) simple
3) complex
4) compound
5) simple
6) compound
7) simple
8) simple
9) complex
10) compound
11) complex
12) simple
13) compound
14) simple
15) complex

Subject/Verb Agreement, page 107

1) has
2) was
3) has
4) were
5) are
6) remains
7) is
8) is
9) was
10) wake

Apostrophes, pages 108–109

1) b. both players' arms
2) d. its culture and its nightlife.
3) a. humankind's earliest inventions.
4) c. one another's basic assumptions and prejudices.
5) c. its hard work

6) b. it's in danger of losing its entire membership

7) a. Egyptian musicians wrote all the music for the movie's soundtrack.

8) d. my horse's back and admired its strength

9) c. The women's soccer team was more successful than the men's team

10) b. Whose mittens are lying on the table?

Commas and Semicolons, pages 110–111

1) d. early morning, just before

2) a. of solving world problems, but she

3) d. late afternoon; however, drinking coffee

4) b. good reputation; she was known

5) c. Trying as hard as she could, the girl still found the rope

6) a. For an entire year, the man ate only soup, salad, and dessert.

7) d. He didn't want to be late; therefore, he would not be.

8) b. The drama club had a tough year ahead, lacking the funding

9) d. The pasta with vegetables, the only vegetarian item on the menu, happened to be

10) c. She wore purple and red to school each day.

Punctuation: Dashes, Colons, Semicolons, Commas, Parentheses, and Ellipses, pages 112–114

1) d

2) c

3) a

4) d

5) c

6) b

7) c

8) c

9) b

10) d

11) ellipsis after wrote and wrote

12) dash after mitt and Jeter

13) parentheses around in case you care to know

14) colon after United States

15) semicolon after paste

Wordiness, page 115

1) She constantly irritates and bothers me.
2) He spoke to me concerning my future.
3) Is it true that the ozone layer is being depleted?
4) Let's go at 2:00 a.m.
5) As a result of the election, the state will have its first female governor.
6) My father's custom is to watch the sun set in the west.
7) At ten years old, Vishal picked up a brush and hasn't stopped painting since.
8) Research shows that avid sports fans not only suffer from depression less, but they are also generally healthier.
9) He is a chemist.
10) For the second time, the cough recurred.

Diction, page 116

1) accepted
2) affect
3) effect
4) than
5) then
6) too
7) their
8) cite
9) may
10) can
11) lay
12) lie
13) sit
14) set
15) fewer
16) less
17) Bring
18) Take
19) among
20) between

Parallelism, pages 117–118

1) d. but also to manage your time well.
2) b. nor write a cover letter for a job application.
3) d. and to maintain its profitability.
4) c. in their school lockers or in their gym lockers.
5) a. but also had to arrange the music for the group.
6) c. nor the lyrics to the song
7) d. both the bride and the groom received welcome baskets
8) Filing taxes is about as much fun as watching paint dry.
9) Cinderella swept the floors, washed the windows, and mopped the kitchen herself.
10) Parents often prefer to pay high school taxes than pay high tuition.
11) Fran spends her free time reading, listening to music, and working in the garden.
12) Students at the college often earn spending money by babysitting and by mowing lawns.

Idioms, page 119

1) I just threw the ball to Diego.
2) I really hope my English teacher will comply with my request for an extra day to write my paper.
3) His ability to understand the problem is different from mine.
4) Because of his preoccupation with traveling all over the world, Justin bought a copy of National Geographic.
5) I am very happy with my friend's behavior.
6) When Lucy returned home, she felt as though she'd never been away.
7) The invaders were horrible people, men who had absolutely no concern with human life.
8) It was definitely impossible for the man to separate reality from fantasy.

Maupin House *by*
capstone
professional

At Maupin House by Capstone Professional, we continue to look for professional development resources that support grades K–8 classroom teachers in areas, such as these:

Literacy	Language Arts
Content-Area Literacy	Research-Based Practices
Assessment	Inquiry
Technology	Differentiation
Standards-Based Instruction	School Safety
Classroom Management	School Community

If you have an idea for a professional development resource, visit our Become an Author website at:

http://maupinhouse.com/index.php/become-an-author

There are two ways to submit questions and proposals.

1. You may send them electronically to:
   http://maupinhouse.com/index.php/become-an-author

2. You may send them via postal mail. Please be sure to include a self-addressed stamped envelope for us to return materials.

Acquisitions Editor
Capstone Professional
1710 Roe Crest Drive
North Mankato, MN 56003